Potomac Review

EDITOR
Albert Kapikian

MANAGING EDITOR
Monica Mische

POETRY EDITOR
Katherine Smith

NONFICTION EDITOR
Viola Clune

ADMINISTRATIVE ASSISTANT/WEBMASTER
Om B. Rusten

ASSOCIATE EDITORS

Conrad Berger
Anjenee Cannon
Theron Coleman
Hieu Duong
Courtney Ford
Robert Giron

Jessie Gouverneur
Michael LeBlanc
Kateema Lee
Alejandro Leopardi
Heather Levine
David Lott

Mike Maggio
Edwin McCleskey
David Saitzeff
Jessie Seigel
Ellen Sullivan
Marianne Szlyk

INTERNS
Susan Boroskin, Frankie Little, Kathryn Mussenden

Potomac Review is a journal of fiction, poetry, and nonfiction
published by the Paul Peck Humanities Institute at
Montgomery College, Rockville
51 Mannakee Street, Rockville, MD 20850

Potomac Review has been made possible through
the generosity of Montgomery College.

A special thanks to Dean Elizabeth Benton.

For submission guidelines and more information:
www.potomacreview.org

Potomac Review, Inc. is a not-for-profit 501 c(3) corp.
Member, Council of Literary Magazines & Presses
Indexed by the American Humanities Index
ISBN: 979-8-9858154-4-3
ISSN: 1073-1989

SUBSCRIBE TO POTOMAC REVIEW

One year at $24 (2 issues)
Two years at $36 (4 issues)

SAMPLE COPY ORDER, $12 (SINGLE ISSUE)

COVER PHOTO

NATIONAL ARBORETUM

BY ROCHELLE COHEN

Table of Contents

NONFICTION

POETRY

POST SCRIPT

NOTES ON ISSUE 75

A community college is a commons tasked with the search for the common interest. Montgomery College, through its literary journal, has been tasked also with the search for another kind of shared resource, an *aesthetic* commons, in a time when it, too, has been hijacked by those who would master it for themselves. *Potomac Review*, now celebrating its 75th issue, continues to signal that open admission is not inconsistent with excellence—its inclusion in the 2024 editions of *Best American Essays* and *Best Spiritual Literature* confirming, once again, that a democratic vision is itself a form of expertise.

The U.S. National Arboretum, in Washington, DC, exemplifies how an aesthetic commons can model democratic vision and excellence, how each can be constitutive of the other, and our cover photograph, taken in the Fall, amidst golden colors and maturing trees, somehow does the same, capturing the place while also defamiliarizing it, offering verisimilitude and at the same time an ecological reading of our *atmospheric* commons. The National Arboretum, where admission is free, offers what the Humanities offers—the kind of education, increasingly abandoned, that does not depend for its significance on some outside factor, that leads nowhere but to itself, not subordinate to some end to which it is but the means.

Higher education is, or should be, a public trust, but we have largely privatized its commons too, and with that, installed a negative soteriology that in a democracy education need not include mutual recognition. The aesthetic forces a commons: people want to be joined *with others*, speak *with others* about what they have seen, read, heard. Our democracy renews itself every four years only to the extent to which the kind of judgment learned in such aesthetic commons are made, judgments made in the context of "the other," of the community.

For Spring 2025, our theme will be "the Other," and one way to envision this theme (there are of course many ways) might be to think about the fostering of connections that renew our aesthetic commons, and therefore, our democracy. If the nation that can be imagined included (and still includes) the National Arboretum, a place where the trees dissolve into otherness, but are *not* cut down, where they blur, like narrative, self and other, then while visiting we can also imagine ourselves permeable and interchangeable in a commons under ecological threat where there is no saving isolation, where the discipline of the other is the only discipline that matters.

There is no higher, harder form of the "wholly other" than the stranger just met, and no greater faith than that given to that same stranger. Still, the necessity of that faith now links all our commons. Our democracy requires learning how to give it; if it did not, we would not be free, and democracy would not be a good. Literature is just such a place for imagined futures, for nation-making narratives where "the other" is also/I, "the unseen" (the theme for our Fall 2025 issue), seen.

Notions of "community," beset by a strong misreading, have become functional, transactional, self-segregating—its manipulators, in the name of "connection," destroying it. Because of this, the call for community implicit in our experiment of self-governance, the care and feeding of the public square implicit in our founding, is being lost; its miracle, which requires husbandry, is being lost because the individual, the individual defined and educated *in the context* of the greater community, is being lost. But here, at the community college, as at the Arboretum, one cannot talk about isolated entities. Here is a commons that does not exist until everyone is invited—arboreal everywhere, unsituated, interfacing amidst *others* in a rhizomatic understory of root entanglement and circulating meaning. The commons itself takes no position—the price of admission only the willingness to look for common ground in the structure that has been made for the American experience, but that can disappear if not modeled for the next generation.

Our experiment in self-government belongs, in the end, to the world of the human spirit, and because of this, it is our great humanists—because they offer specific and concrete attention to the questions of government and reveal the ways that the human spirit is not always infallible in matters of the polis and public life—who are also, by definition, our great pedagogues. We cannot foresee the circumstances our next generations will encounter, but we can equip them with the tools with which they will encounter them.

Language circulates in a commons, so literary originality exists only in its context, with no boundary between form and social discourse. Since *Potomac Review*'s creation, in 1993, by its founder and first editor, Eli Flam, and subsequent connection, in 2001, to Montgomery College, and a succession of editors—Christa Watters, Julie Wakeman-Linn, Zachary Benavidez, and John Wang—who have, through their connection to the circumstances that produce it, shown how literary form, by submitting to the discipline of the other, can itself create a commons of excellence.

I RECKON WITH MY FEET

THE first time a girl witnesses her toes in the mouth of another, she would not have anticipated it happening during a game at church. It is complicated. I use that word in its oldest sense: entangled, combined, intertwined. Not tongue in cheek. No, big toe carving into the soft pink. I stood on a blue tarp—the brightest one you could imagine—so creased and dry. I stood in a line with other children who were picked to participate in the game. They challenged us to make an icecream sundae with our feet. If you have attended church camp, you are familiar with these disgusting antics. There is always a hint of the grotesque in children's games: ashes, ashes, we all fall down.

The organizers of the event had already filled the bowl with icecream. My responsibility was to arrange the toppings with my toes. Using my big toe and less so special second toe, I clipped the banana in half, picked out cherries close to bursting. Do not ask me how I put the chocolate syrup in the bowl. Were there small bowls with spoons that I had to wield? All I can recall it that I finished the sundae and dashed, feet covered in chocolate, to my partner seated at the table.

With the sundae in front of them, they supped. Ate what I had made to the audience's amusement and disgust. I recall one young man running toward a large trash can, one that you would see in a school cafeteria, and hurling up his lunch. The first team to finish would receive a prize most coveted: an iTunes giftcard, a plastic ticket to music paradise. Not to my surprise, my team was the first to finish, but the game did not end there.

I was a teenager when I realized some sects of Christianity believed in raw transmutation. They did not hold a tasteless wafer and Kroger grape juice in their hands; no, this was truly the body and blood. This surprised me as the faith of Pentecostals could surely will such a transformation. After all, we believed in lying with the spirit, feeling it sink into our bones until a marathon could be run, the arrival of a different tongue in our mouths, a message could be conceived in such mayhem. My cheek became intimately familiar with the green Church of God carpet; the gum-stuck, wax-touched, tear-strung carpet. How easy it is to lower oneself.

They chose volunteers from the crowd. My partner was the young man who had thrown up his lunch. He had a biblical name, of course, one that meant miracle. The man in charge, balding and bellied, gave our partners a single challenge, to suck the chocolate clean off of our toes. Did I feel horror or shock? Curiosity? Pleasure? I retain to this day an image of that young man, Miracle's golden hair and the memory of lips closing around my pinky toe, propped up on his elbows. How warm my cheeks were. We did not win the gift card, that I know for sure. I would illegally torrent a Casting Crowns album months later and get my family's internet shut off.

Could the grotesque appear as a need for penitence? On the pastel pink and blue tiles of the church kitchen, colored like those chalky Easter mints, we consumed decadent concoctions. These were lock-ins (meant to be pray-ins) but in adolescence, you want to talk to boys, not God. Around a blender we would stand, dropping in ingredients without relent: ketchup, candy, whatever was available in the church pantry. Gross was our brand of charity. The chunky scarlet celebration turned in serrated circles—of course it was red, it had to be. Now, drink. God was watching, teased the other kids. You had to drink. Drinking became a way of knowing.

It was the same for Margareta. She lived long before me: cross kisser, a sister-disser. Mystics talked shit like it was a requirement. She was upset. I wish I could tell you that she knelt on tiles or carpet or what her knees looked like. What is known is that she wept. She wanted to kiss it: that large cross that hung in the sanctuary, but she could not reach it. So Christ came to her in a dream and bared his breast. Drink, he said.

And she drank till she was blood drunk. We put our mouths on wounds to seal them. Could it be that Margareta was healing him while he was nourishing her?

I think the same of my cut finger mingling with my tongue. I prefer my verbs to have a color. Wondering is a red string. If you do the right movements, you can make a ladder. Use a pointer finger to pick up the strings from each palm. Drop the pinkies. Drop the thumbs. Keep picking up strings. This next part is tricky. Don't pull too tight. A little tension is good; you don't want too much. Your hands will have to pass through these small shapes. You will need to turn your hands away from you to see it: the ladder from which God and his angels will descend and ascend. A ladder made by your hands. Touching, healing, and writing: little girl, they're all red.

THE HOUSE OF MOURNING

I

THE Old Man wanted to see him. Henry Vanderburgh, knocking on Alfred Beach's door, worried that a client had complained, although he couldn't make out whom he'd disappointed or disconcerted. He was relieved when his employer asked him to look over the proofs for the October 6th issue. Beach had edited *Scientific American* for nearly fifty years and had cofounded with Orson Munn the most important firm of patent attorneys in the United States, but still stood expectantly, hands clasped behind his back, waiting to hear Henry's response.

Henry examined the articles: The Fort Wayne Electric Corporation— Its Dynamos and General Electric Lighting Apparatus; A Velocipede to Run on Snow and Ice; Easily Read Thermometers; and Mr. Maxim's Flying Machine. Hiram Maxim's enormous biplane, launched on the grounds of his estate in Bexley in front of an audience including Prince Albert of Wales, flew three hundred yards through the air – astonishing. There was also an article on the Pleiades star cluster by Professor William Payne from Carleton College.

"What a wonderful issue," Henry said.

"It really is, isn't it? One of our best. Sit down, my boy."

So there was something else after all. Henry sat stiffly, careful not to dislodge the embroidered antimacassars on the arms and back of the armchair facing Beach's desk. Behind Beach was a large window with its panoramic view of lower Manhattan.

The Old Man was of middle height, with carefully parted gray hair and a thin gray mustache under his broad nose. His chin dipped inward briefly before protruding outward. The large nose and bulbous chin, along with Orson Munn's thicket of sideburns and Charles Munn's neatly manicured walrus mustache with its waxed tips, were featured prominently in the Thomas Nast-inspired caricatures of management drawn by the office staff of Munn & Company, Attorneys at Law. Henry took care to keep his brown hair and his mustache clipped, lest he invite similar ridicule. He knew he probably worried too much. He was only a few years out of law school and hardly part of management.

Still, he hated attracting attention – a family legacy, Henry supposed. His father, Thomas Vanderburgh, had hated notice of any kind. He found it vulgar.

"I've come to learn, never mind how, that you've been dining lately with a Miss Caroline Wilkes at Sherry's."

Henry found he was gripping his knees. New York society was certainly small and insular, and he worried Beach would bring up the Walter Sides, Jr. situation. What business was it to the Old Man whom Henry chose to take out for supper, anyway? "Yes."

"I understand she's very beautiful."

"She is," Henry replied at once.

"And has she quite captured your heart?"

But this question was more difficult to answer. "Perhaps she's on the way to capturing it, sir."

"You hardly need my encouragement, but I think it would be a propitious step for you to wed. Men who live alone too long can become —peculiar," Beach said.

Henry knew his employer was thinking about his cofounder's son. Charles Munn was ten years older than Henry, in his late thirties, and had never married, but seemed to prefer the company of the handsome young men with whom he played polo, golf, tennis, and racquets. Henry considered another peculiar bachelor, his father's first cousin James Vanderburgh Parker, who insisted on driving his four-in-hand carriage through clogged Manhattan streets. Lately Parker had taken up with a married woman from Provincetown.

Not that the Old Man should cast stones. Beach was odd himself, with his enduring obsession with a pneumatic subway, a system he had patented. The first electric underground line was about to open but the

Old Man held out hopes for his invention and kept a model of a Beach Pneumatic Transit train car in his office. The model had its role in the office caricatures, too: sometimes Beach wore the train as a bowtie in the cartoons.

"I think, if you were to marry, we'd raise your salary," Beach said.

"Thank you."

"Two can't live as cheaply as one, contrary to what many believe. And if Miss Wilkes is as lovely as people say, well, you'll want to show her off a bit. That costs money."

"I suppose so," Henry said. But Caroline wasn't a figurine to be admired by gawkers and the gauche, like the latest novelty at the Schwarz Toy Bazaar in Union Square.

"Life has its inevitable vicissitudes and disappointments." And here, inevitably indeed, Beach glanced at his model subway train. "A man needs a helpmeet to face them. Marriage has its vagaries, too, but my boy, you'll find you can get through almost anything if you share the same values."

Life advice from the Old Man; Henry hadn't expected that. But what he found pressing wasn't so much the counsel as the need to speak with his stepmother, Lillian. If the news that Henry was courting Caroline had reached Beach, then Lillian must have heard as well. He didn't know why he hadn't discussed Miss Wilkes with her yet. Surely she'd be happy for him. He stopped at her home on Irving Place – his home, although he didn't live there any longer; legally it belonged to the trust established for him in his father's will, and Henry was forbidden to sell or otherwise dispose of it – and walked up one side of the curved and ornate split staircase leading to the entrance. The three-story, Italianate brownstone was not so imposing as the staircase seemed to suggest. Like its tall windows, the building was rather narrow and, hemmed in by trees and neighboring row houses on either side, rather dark as well.

The Irish maid said she would see if Mrs. Vanderburgh was in. He heard murmured voices and then the soft flurry of footsteps heading upstairs, and he wondered, not for the first time, if Lillian only dressed in black when he visited. The maid returned and said his stepmother would be down in a few minutes.

Lillian had livened the drawing room with a decorative mantel over the fireplace, light wood tea tables and chairs for playing bezique, and the pastel palette she'd chosen for the carpets, curtains, and upholstery. It was here that his stepmother greeted him. She received him with her usual smile and a quick peck on the cheek.

"An unexpected treat."

"I was walking in the neighborhood and decided to try my luck and see if you were home."

Lillian was amused. "Your chances were certainly good on a Tuesday morning. But you can see me anytime, you know that." Meaning, she was always home.

She was in her thirties, with a comely face and a fine outline, as Thomas Vanderburgh would have put it, dark-haired, light-eyed, smooth-browed, and far too young, Henry thought, to cloister herself in this dark house on Irving Place.

"When is Jennie back?"

"All Saint's Day. I'll have her home for a full week. Another treat."

"Then you're quite alone," Henry said.

"I don't mind." Meaning, she minded.

He knew her well, could tell what she was thinking just as she knew what he was hiding. He presumed that she didn't visit friends often because she couldn't afford to entertain in return. His father, whose meanness lived on even after his death, had left Lillian a meager inheritance and nothing at all to Jennie. The capital for Henry was tied up in the unbreachable trust. Some dividends, at least, dribbled down to him.

"I'm sorry I haven't been here to visit you more often, but I must confess, I've been distracted lately."

"Distracted?"

"In the most entertaining and delightful way. By a young lady."

"Oh yes?" Meaning, she already knew. "How wonderful."

"A Miss Caroline Wilkes."

"Wilkes… Is she related by chance to Sarah Wilkes Cushing of Tuxedo Park?" Meaning, she knew exactly whom he was wooing. Her cousins, or her friend Mary Lorillard Barbey, or who knew, perhaps the mayor or the Irish maid had heard the gossip and hurried to inform her.

"Her sister."

"I remember, Sarah Wilkes was very good-looking. If Caroline Wilkes has caught your fancy, then might I assume there's a family resemblance?" She was smiling at him again.

His stepmother was good-looking herself. It was no wonder that his father had pursued her.

"I haven't had the pleasure of making Mrs. Cushing's acquaintance yet, but they do say both girls take after their mother," Henry said. "And Mrs. Wilkes was known as a great beauty in her time."

"Well, then Harry, I'm not the least bit surprised that you've been distracted."

Only his stepmother called him Harry, her pet name for him when he was a boy. "Harry" because it almost rhymed with "scary," and she claimed that he had intimidated her at first. Only later did he realize that she feigned her fear to reassure him. He was fifteen when his father remarried, and Lillian was twenty-five, closer in age to Henry than to her husband.

"You must bring her to the house," Lillian said. "As soon as possible."

Henry presented an envelope with cash for Jennie. Lillian demurred accepting it, but Henry insisted. "I just received a dividend from the B&O," he lied. His father had invested in railroad stocks like the Baltimore and Ohio, that much was true, but Henry's dividends had been slashed since the Panic began the previous year. "It gives me pleasure to share it with her."

Lillian reluctantly took the envelope.

"Then it's settled," Lillian said as he was leaving. "Sunday afternoon. I can't wait to meet her. We'll be sure to discuss your foibles and embarrass you terribly."

Miss Wilkes was looking forward to meeting his stepmother as well, sensing this marked a further development of her relations with Henry. She took the opportunity of buying a new day dress at Lord & Taylor and asked Henry if she could model it for him. The dress was azalea pink and made of silk, with a square neckline, a corseted waist, a matching overskirt à la polonaise, and a sash belt. It was certainly lovely, although perhaps elaborate for a casual visit.

But Caroline – she really was ravishing. How had Walter Sides, Jr. parted with such a delightful creature?

"You like it?"

"Very much," he said. The Old Man was right after all, she should be shown off in a dress like that. He stared frankly at the square neckline of the dress. A man's head can be turned by a pretty woman: another of his father's admonitions. But maybe, for once, he wanted his head to be turned, wanted to escape – what?

"You're scaring me," Caroline said with a smile.

Lost in thought, he'd been staring at her too long, and now he smiled too, to reassure her.

"You can't blame me for looking."

"Look but don't touch," said her mother, who had overheard them.

Henry and Caroline's eyes met, and they laughed.

AFTER his father died, Henry had thought it might look improper if he continued to live with his attractive stepmother. He told Lillian that he intended to relocate uptown to be closer to his friends and his clubs. In reality, he wanted her to feel comfortable remaining in the house, where she wouldn't have to pay rent. He'd taken a bachelor flat at the Wilbraham, a new eight story building at the corner of Fifth Avenue and 30th Street with a copper-covered roof and electric lighting.

Henry had explained to Caroline that although the house had been left in trust to him, his stepmother resided there. Caroline was touched by his generosity – but Mrs. Vanderburgh couldn't expect to live there forever, could she? It wasn't fair to Henry and certainly his stepmother must hate imposing on him so much. Now that her daughter was away in boarding school, she could live in simpler quarters.

They walked together in the mellow October afternoon to Irving Place. The oppressive heat of the summer had lifted, and the beauty of the trees with their changing leaves, the blooming asters, and the autumn crocus pleased the eye just as the gentle sun warmed the skin.

The social season would start soon, in November. They had just been invited to a dinner party at the home of Mr. and Mrs. Charles "Carley" Havemeyer, of the Havemeyer Sugar Trust family. Havemeyer, usually cheerful although like Henry sometimes subject to melancholia, was a good friend. Unfortunately, his marriage was not known to be a happy one. The Havemeyers belonged to the upper echelon of Manhattan society, and Caroline was excited to be included.

Margaret had Sundays off, and his stepmother let them in. After some polite chit-chat in the drawing room, and after Miss Wilkes declined any coffeecake as she was watching her figure, the young woman asked to see the rest of the house and Mrs. Vanderburgh took her on a tour. Caroline professed to adore it. She said that the townhouse had excellent bones, that it would be a good first home for a couple before their family expanded and they needed more room. She wondered if they'd considered installing a skylight over the interior stairs to let in more light, and perhaps another oriel window in the third floor façade. Henry's stepmother smiled indulgently.

Caroline proceeded through the house, offering her various recommendations: lantern shades from Macy's for the gas lamps, a rocker for the nursery, they were on sale for $2.15 at Bloomingdale's on Third Avenue, a new carpet in the drawing room. W. and J. Sloane were selling Oriental rugs; the carpets were expensive, but they would last a lifetime. At Stern Brothers they had an adorable infant's basket with a tufted silk center and silk lining for $7.98.

She knew the Brothers, Louis Stern was a friend of her grandfather.

She had certainly done her research. "Carrie," Henry murmured, trying to get her to stop.

His stepmother's smile was tighter now. "No, please go on."

Caroline described the changes she would make if she were living there. The curtains – Lillian's favorite curtains in the drawing room – might need an update and B. Altman was having a sale. Her grandfather was friends with Benjamin Altman, too. As for housewares, Caroline preferred Hilton, Hughes & Company.

She left the house on Irving Place in fine spirits. Henry was sure the visit had been a disaster.

II

His mother died when he was thirteen. Henry had no siblings and he and his mother had been close. Sometimes she was highly active and high-spirited, sleeping fitfully if at all, and full of passionate plans. Sometimes, lugubrious, she withdrew to her bedroom. But even when she was downcast, she drew Henry to her side so that they might snuggle. It was as if, he sometimes thought, they'd sensed that they wouldn't have much time together.

Henry was an excitable boy, charging through the hallways of the house on Irving Place, shouting commands to his imaginary army, routing Napoleon or the Confederates, incapable of quieting himself down. Or, like his mother unaccountably disconsolate, he would withdraw to his room, quiet and sullen, comforting himself with books and almanacs, marveling at the ancient Egyptian's engineering of the pyramids at Giza and the latest scientific advances. His mood swings infuriated his father who insisted he learn to behave himself and who read to him from exhortatory tracts on thrift, industry, and self-control.

His father must have loved Henry's mother too, Henry reasoned, because he changed after her death. It was then that the Biblical readings started – Ecclesiastes, mostly, but not so much the eat, drink, and be merry passages as the various admonishments. His father was especially fond of one verse: The heart of the wise is in the house of mourning, but the heart of fools is in the house of mirth. As if Henry didn't know already that he was living in the house of mourning.

His father respected learned professors, scrupulous accountants, and beautiful women who lived within their means, but little else. He certainly didn't respect his son, who disappointed him first with his rowdiness, now with his prolonged melancholy.

Little by little his stepmother brought him out of his depression, with her nicknames for him, her playfulness, and her teasing. Almost at once there sprung up between the boy and Lillian a mysterious bond. They were like mother and son, sitting close together in the family room and sharing confidences; they were like brother and sister, laughing at private jokes and plotting against their strict father; they were like mischievous friends, looking to make trouble and sneaking into the liquor cabinet without getting caught. And superadded to these relations was something else, a sentimental attachment that both felt but couldn't define. She even shared his interest in Egyptology.

She was shrewd, very shrewd. And patient, too. As his father was opposed to changing the furniture or atmosphere of the house, Lillian's alterations were imperceptible at first. Slowly, so slowly that his father couldn't object or even notice, she was able to take possession of a single room on each story. First the drawing room on the first floor, where she entertained her lady friends for card games or kaffeeklatsches; then an intimate family sitting room on the second floor, the friendliest space in the house as it was lit up by the bay window, a cheerful chandelier, and, when it was cold enough for Thomas Vanderburgh to countenance, a fire blazing in the fireplace; and finally, Jennie's room on the top floor. Jennie, who arrived at Irving Place when she was only three years old, was a great and unexpected gift to an only child. She idolized Henry and he was devoted to her in turn. At times she was sister to him, at times nearly a daughter.

When he graduated from law school, his father hoped that he would join him at Carter, Hughes, & Cravath, where Thomas Vanderburgh practiced law, but Henry didn't want to be indebted to his father nor under his surveillance. He sought and won a position at Munn & Company as it better suited his interests. The scientists and inventors he represented were changing the course of history, and he negotiated with patent agents in London, Paris, Madrid, Hong Kong, and Calcutta. The whole world was at his feet. He loved his work. It sustained him.

III

LILLIAN sent him a note asking him to call on her. Henry procrastinated as long as possible, but at last the feared encounter could be delayed no longer. The sun was setting as he walked from his office on Wall Street to Irving Place. The electric lights on Fifth Avenue, still a novelty to him, gleamed yellow in the gathering darkness. He rehearsed his responses in advance. He was old enough to make his own decisions. Caroline meant no harm, she was just exuberant, she took after his mother in that way. Lillian could stay in the house as long as she wanted.

Margaret let him in, ushering him to the charmless parlor, presumably according to Mrs. Vanderburgh's instructions. The gas lamps cast a sickly light over the dark furniture. His stepmother came down the stairs, elegant in one of her borrowed black dresses. This time she offered him a hand, not a kiss.

"Thank you for coming," she said.

"Of course."

They sat down for tea, and both felt the strain as they avoided the matter at hand, talking instead about Jennie, home soon for the first of November, about the weather, about Cousin James Parker's latest peccadilloes. Parker had always been a particular favorite of his stepmother.

"Miss Wilkes is quite charming," Lillian finally began.

"She liked you, too. Very much."

"And she's certainly very beautiful. Like her sister Sarah, as I expected."

"Thank you."

"But I must say, she's not whom I imagined you marrying." Lillian's brow wrinkled, as though to suggest perplexity.

"Really? How so?"

"I'm not sure you share quite the same values."

Values again, as the Old Man had preached. "I don't follow," Henry said.

"Well, you've never been guided by money, not really. And she's certainly very commercially minded, don't you think? She seems to know the price of everything. I imagine that's been passed down to her from her ancestors. That ability with money, it can be a gift, I suppose."

Henry understood that she was referring, and far from obliquely, to

Caroline's maternal grandfather, a Jew from Austria who had converted. But this was strange behavior for his stepmother. She'd never cut Mrs. Therese Schiff or Mrs. Harriet Lehman if she chanced upon them during one of her infrequent excursions to Lord & Taylor or Arnold Constable, and she was family friends with Fredericka Belmont Howland, a socialite, whose father was a German Jew.

In any case, Caroline's ancestry hadn't hindered her sister from making an advantageous marriage.

"And then, I hate to be indelicate," she said, now with a pained expression on her face, "but there's the Walter Sides, Jr. situation that we have to consider."

Like Caroline, his stepmother had done her research. "It's not like you to respond to gossip."

"You're angry with me."

"No," Henry said. "Disappointed."

Walter Sides, Jr. had courted Caroline assiduously then suddenly dropped her, probably under pressure from his parents. That was Caroline's perspective, and Henry believed her. The Sides family made out that Caroline had schemed to marry Walter, spreading rumors that they were to be engaged in order to compromise him, and that Walter had narrowly escaped her manipulations. It was probably true that Caroline had got ahead of herself, assuming a commitment from Walter that hadn't been formally offered, but this expectancy wasn't based on Caroline's flight of fancy, but rather on Walter's sedulous attentions.

"I have to be both mother and father to you," Lillian said.

"Not really. You don't hold either position."

He'd been harsh with her, and she considered her response for a moment. "All right. Then I trust you'll allow me to call myself a friend. And as a friend I must tell you that I can't approve of this union. I know you may find this hard to forgive, but I owe it to my love for you to be truthful. She's not the proper companion for you. She's too eager to spend her family's money and yours, she lacks depth, and from all accounts she's too open with her affections." These last charges struck him with almost physical force. Caroline was deemed a spendthrift, a flibbertigibbet, and a flirt, all based on a single meeting and overheard innuendo?

"You're a serious person, Henry, you need a serious wife," Lillian concluded.

BREAK off with Caroline? Preposterous. The affrontery of his stepmother's attack – the indecency of it. Carrie was a wonderful girl... Choked with rage, he walked blindly to Union Square and then up Broadway past Madison Square Park, barely noticing his surroundings until he came to 39th Street and stood across the street from the Moorish facade of the Casino Theater.

A few years earlier he had seen Gilbert and Sullivan's *The Yeoman of the Guard* at the Casino. The audience hadn't liked the operetta with its unhappy ending – two barely tolerated marriage proposals and the despair of a scorned, broken-hearted jester – but Henry had loved the production. For weeks afterward he had found himself singing "I Have a Song to Sing, O!", one of his favorite melodies from the show:

> It's a song of a merryman, moping mum,
> Whose soul was sad, and whose glance was glum,
> Who sipped no sup, and who craved no crumb,
> As he sighed for the love of a lady.

Was he then the bereft Jack Point, the strolling jester, condemned to collapse insensible at the feet of his beloved?

Except – except he wasn't bereft. That's what he had to admit to himself, that's what infuriated him most of all. What if Lillian was right? Carrie was too quick to spend money, and it was clear that she was planning to spend much more. Even if she imagined these were all wedding presents from her father, well, he hadn't wanted to be beholden to his own father, he certainly didn't want to be beholden to hers.

Didn't he want to marry a woman, yes, a beautiful woman, who lived within her means? It was also true that she had given him her affection rather quickly. Was he only – his great fear – a quick replacement for Walter Sides, Jr.? Was she trying to scrub off the stink of her social embarrassment, believing that marriage with any eligible gentleman would cleanse her reputation? An attorney from an old Dutch family and the owner of a house on Irving Place, yes, that checked the box, that would certainly do.

Did they, in the end, share the same values? Not really. She cared about social status and pretty clothing as anyone might, but what else? Did they speak of education, their hopes for the future, the Panic and Coxey's Army, impressionism and art nouveau, the latest scientific advances? Or even Gilbert and Sullivan and *Pudd'nhead Wilson*?

Break off with Caroline? He had to.

CAROLINE crumpled to the floor, her satin dress billowing around her and rippling with the heaves of her sobbing.

She cried, "I despise you. I wish I could die."

She cried, "I'll show you one day, I'll make you suffer like you've made me suffer. You'll see, you'll beg me to come back, and then I'll laugh. I'll laugh in your face because I loathe you so much."

She cried, "But I still love you. What did I do to deserve this?"

She cried, "Why are you so cruel? Why can't you let me love you? It costs you nothing. Nothing at all. My parents have money, they'll give it to us, it could be yours."

She cried, "It would be so wonderful, the two of us. We could travel, to Rome, to Cairo, you said you wanted to see the pyramids, I'll go anywhere you want, and I can pay for it, just let me go with you."

She cried, "You're despicable. Oh my God, it hurts. One day you'll understand. But it will be too late, and I won't forgive you. You'll see."

She cried, "Don't leave me."

IV

SPRING came and many of the Four Hundred decamped for Paris. Those who remained, needing to fill seats at dinner parties, remembered Mrs. Vanderburgh, poor thing, who'd been left next to nothing by her husband. Lillian was invited as well to Mary Barbey's second home in Tuxedo Park, and even to Cousin James's Sans Souci in Newport, already open for the summer by May. Henry was invited out less often, except by the Carley Havemeyers, as he was deemed eccentric with his interest in elevators and electricity, new mining techniques, safety boilers, and other contraptions. His charitable work was important, Society reckoned, but dull.

Esteemed by the Munns and Alfred Beach, however, and working long hours after the break-up, Henry assumed greater responsibilities at the law firm. The Old Man had come to rely on him, and he was sent for several weeks to the branch office in Washington, D.C. when Munn & Company were short-staffed there. During his stay, Lillian obtained an invitation for him for dinner at the Howlands' residence in the capital, where he met a woman, Ida Fletcher.

Ida was from Philadelphia and had mutual friends with the Howlands, who had taken an interest in her. She was not so thin nor as attractive as Caroline and considerably less affluent, and she was Henry's senior by a few years – nearly an old maid at thirty. What she possessed instead of youth, wealth, and great beauty was an innate charm, a musical laugh (she laughed often), and a wonderful enthusiasm. She had dark brown hair, brown eyes that danced when she was amused, a dark complexion with hints of auburn red in her cheeks and mouth. She was buxom and wide in her hips, not slender not tall enough for the wasp-waisted Gibson Girl ideal, but she wore a vivid lavender dress that complemented her skin tone, and Henry was drawn at once to her. Sensing his earnestness, she began immediately to tease him, making fun of his love of the law and his do-goodery with the Red Cross, but it was a tender chaffing that suggested she respected the very things she was teasing him about. To be admired and teased simultaneously: delicious.

Carley Havemeyer had asked Henry to come with him to inspect the Sugar Trust's new refinery in Philadelphia, extracted from a rival after a bitter price war. As he had business with clients in the city, Henry was able to join his friend. He had written to Ida and asked if he could accompany her to a meal. They dined together several times, at Wanamaker's tea room, where Ida entertained him with stories of her boisterous childhood in Colorado and Arizona mining towns before her father was ruined, and at the Continental Hotel on Chestnut Street, where they feasted on Little Neck clams, spring lamb with mint sauce, croquettes of sweetbread with peas, and orange méringue pie for dessert. Henry was glad to see her enjoy her appetite after Caroline's abstemiousness.

Ida wanted to travel to Europe, but as the trip was beyond her means, she was waiting for an opportunity to serve as a companion to someone taking the Grand Tour. She loved architecture especially and hoped to visit Florence to see Brunelleschi's Duomo, Giotto's campanile, and Michelangelo's Laurentian Library.

He visited her again in Philadelphia, and she visited him in New York, accompanied by her mother. Mrs. Fletcher's face was etched with worry lines. She had been through too much, the move to rough, lonely mining communities, the shame of her husband's bankruptcy, the difficulties with their son. Rumors of their troubles had followed them back to Pennsylvania. Ida's marriage prospects had been dashed by the irregularities associated with her father and brother— although perhaps they might recover with the patronage of the Howlands; her parents certainly hoped so. This, anyway, was what Henry had gathered. He had done his research, too.

In June at the Pennsylvania Academy of Fine Arts they stood a long while in front of Whistler's controversial *Arrangement in Black (The Lady in the Yellow Buskin)*. Was the subject a haughty aristocrat, wearing modish boots and disdainfully holding a yellow glove, or a harlot, a common streetwalker casting a backward glance toward a potential client? That the woman could be mistaken for both gave the work its frisson.

In July, with Ida's mother as chaperone, they took a ferry from Manhattan to the Clason Point resort at the southern tip of the Annexed District of the Bronx. They picnicked on cold roasted chicken and lemonade, they shared a paper sack of Saratoga chips. When Mrs. Fletcher was pretending not to watch, they took off their shoes and dipped their toes in the East River at the bathing pier. They held hands and his heart swelled. He loved Ida. What he had experienced with Caroline paled in comparison to this new relation. He had been infatuated with Caroline, nothing more. Now he knew the real thing.

THE Old Man, during a rare vacation in Newport, had met Henry's stepmother at Sans Souci. Beach, who considered himself an expert on women and fashion, extolled Mrs. Vanderburgh's appearance. She was wearing a lustrous cinnamon-orange tea gown of chiffon velvet with gigot sleeves, he recalled, somewhat low at the décolletage, with a lace collar. A French design, he assumed, probably House of Worth and probably a few years old, which was seemlier and less ostentatious than wearing fashion from the current season. "No corset, she doesn't need one. A fine figure of a woman." He approved.

Henry went to see his stepmother to tell her that he intended to marry Ida. Lillian wore black when they conferred in the drawing room and when Ida, like Caroline, was invited to an afternoon tea at Irving Place. His stepmother was still wearing black when she summoned Henry for a meeting. But she couldn't object to Ida, Henry thought, as Ida had behaved impeccably.

"She's not so prepossessing as Miss Wilkes," Lillian observed.

"No, but lovely in her own way."

"And she's quite serious, isn't she."

Henry, tense, found he was gripping his knees again. "Not always. But you disparaged Miss Wilkes's lack of seriousness, as I recall."

"I have to tell you, I'm worried," Lillian said.

"Why?"

"The Fletchers' history."

"Mrs. Howland has no such reservations," Henry countered.

"Mrs. Howland is a generous woman, and she pities Ida. It's bad enough what the father did. But the brother…"

"That was ten years ago."

"It's still fresh in people's minds."

He was no longer surprised by his stepmother's ability to unearth whatever facts were needed to support her arguments. After Mr. Fletcher's mining investments had collapsed in 1884, during the previous Panic, Ida's brother had stolen funds from the bank where he worked, trying to pay off his father's creditors. The bank hadn't wanted any publicity that might scare away their already skittish customers, and the embezzlement was hushed up as the Fletchers borrowed from relatives to reimburse the stolen money and left the territory. Over time this sordid history had come to light in Philadelphia and now New York.

"It doesn't seem fair that Ida is being punished for other people's mistakes."

"I wish it wasn't the case. But wishing won't make it so. You'll be ostracized, Harry," Lillian said.

"I don't believe that."

She looked at him and Henry thought that her eyes filled with pity. Or was she playacting? "You could lose your job."

"No. Mr. Beach depends on me."

"And the fiduciaries might decide you were violating the morality clause of the trust."

Was she threatening him? He couldn't imagine that the officers of the Guaranty Trust Company cared whom he married, if she bore no personal responsibility for any malfeasance.

"I'll have to take that chance," he told her.

HE worried that the Old Man would call him in for another tête-à-tête, but it was Charles Munn who invited him for drinks at his home. Henry had forgotten that Charles knew his stepmother. They were the same age and had attended cotillions together when they were young. Munn's townhouse on East 65th Street was impeccably furnished. When not sporting with his lusty friends, Charles collected portraits of George Washington and colonial silverware.

"Mrs. Vanderburgh was quite right to contact me," he told Henry. "You understand that we can't tolerate any hint of misconduct at Munn & Company. I'm afraid you'd be implicated if you wed Miss Fletcher."

His stepmother had gone for the jugular. "And sir, you understand that she is completely innocent of any wrongdoing. This is guilt by association. It wouldn't stand up in a court of law."

"I'm not talking about the court of law but the court of popular opinion. We simply can't have it, old boy. If you were to marry this girl, you'd have to leave."

Leave Munn & Company? His job was everything to him.

"Of course, we'd bear you no ill will," Charles Munn said, "and we'd give you a sound recommendation for future employers. But I imagine they'd be hesitant as well."

THAT night Henry felt the old pain returning. Usually he could fight his depression, busying himself during the day with legal work, filling his evenings with club events, fundraising for the Red Cross, and theater and opera productions. But he didn't think he could manage if his job was taken away. The rest wouldn't suffice, not even with Ida accompanying him.

He walked all night long. He hadn't escaped, in the end. The house of mourning accompanied and encased him everywhere he went. Like a turtle, he thought, like an ugly turtle that was always at home in its shell. He sang softly to himself:

> Heighdy! heighdy!
> Misery me, lackadaydee!
> He sipped no sup, and he craved no crumb,
> As he sighed for the love of a lady.

He looked up at the sky, searching futilely for the Pleiades. In his article on the star cluster, Professor Payne had quoted the Book of Job. Canst thou bind the sweet influences of the Pleiades? Or loose the bands of Orion? Henry felt no sweet influence, no fatherly or motherly advice to guide him, only the bands of anxiety that were tightening around his chest.

In the morning, still without having slept, he called upon James Parker. His cousin agreed to see him and Henry, fatigued and therefore less restrained, poured out his story. His cousin lived without seeking or requiring society's approbation, could Henry do the same?

Parker looked at him, genuinely confused. "But my child, you don't have the income."

IDA cried softly on her chair. Henry had come to Philadelphia to break the news to her.

She said, "Don't talk like that. You don't mean what you say."

She said, "Don't leave me. Please don't go."

She said, "You know how I really feel. You've been lonely in your life, too." She said, "I never meant to harm you."

V

HE wasn't the same; he'd never be the same. He missed Ida terribly.

Three years passed. Lillian had become a passionate Dreyfusard. She read *Le Petit Journal* at the home of James Parker, who imported the Paris newspapers. There or at Sans Souci she met Parker's friend Robert Underwood, the retired American consul for Alexandria, Egypt, now a major investor in the Buffalo, Rochester, and Pittsburgh railway. Lillian married him and moved into his house, a newly built mansion, after they honeymooned in France and Italy. The property on Irving Place was temporarily vacant.

News reached Henry that Ida had married Edward Granville, a man of limited means and even more limited intelligence. He was just smart enough, Henry surmised, to know that he needed a smart wife to guide him. Granville, hoping for a career in politics or the foreign service, was angling for a post with the State Department, and the Howlands' connections in Washington would help him. Apparently the State Department had no objections to Ida's history. Henry knew Granville slightly. He could have wished for a more substantive husband for Ida, but he understood that in breaking off with her, he had damaged her already weakened position in the marketplace.

He had damaged his own reputation as well. Young women were wary of a man who had disappointed two brides-to-be. He was alone, and he still longed for Ida. At least at work he was busy; the Panic had finally subsided and the economy was booming. He saw the latest Ibsen play, *John Gabriel Borkman*, at Hoyt's Theater and the American premiere of *Manon* at the Met. He raised money for Clara Barton and the victims of the Hamidian massacres. He had given up attending dinner parties, even the Carley Havemeyers'. At night he read the weekly *Scientific American* or Professor Petrie's published reports on his archaeological dig at Tanis. And none of it, not the plays, not the operas, not the reading, made him miss Ida any less.

He was becoming, Henry supposed, another peculiar, confirmed bachelor.

His stepmother sent him a note, asking to see him. He called on Mrs. Underwood at her new Riverside Drive residence. A butler let him in. It was a five story building of light brick and limestone, and with its oversized dormer windows and mansard roof, it resembled a Parisian mansion. Lillian must love the windows, Henry thought, which let light pour into the vast interiors.

She received Henry in the music room, more intimate than the parlor, Lillian assured him. Overhead were electric chandeliers in the shape of Queen Anne's Lace, designed by Louis Comfort Tiffany. Margaret, who had accompanied Lillian to the Upper West Side, brought them a small silver tray with a Waterford sherry crystal decanter and two petite sherry glasses which she rested on a rosewood side table. They would have a drink before tea, Lillian explained. He thought that she'd been drinking already.

She sipped her sherry. "I was visiting Mrs. Barbey in Tuxedo Park, and I ran into Miss Wilkes there."

"Oh?"

"She asked after you. After you, most especially."

He reached reflexively to clasp his knees but stopped himself. "I hope Caroline's well."

"She is. And she's certainly still beautiful. But I must say, there's a greater maturity to her now. And I also must say," Mrs. Underwood's hands were trembling slightly, "I think I misjudged her. I was too harsh, and for that, I'm truly sorry."

"Perhaps it wasn't meant to be."

"She wants to see you, Harry."

"I find that hard to believe," he said evenly.

"It's true." She finished her drink. "I would like to invite her here for luncheon one afternoon and I'd like you to join us. If you'll permit me. A quiet meal. Nothing very elaborate."

He gestured at the chandeliers. "I find that hard to believe, too."

She smiled. "Well, I'll do my best. May I, Harry? Scary Harry?"

"I think we've established that it's hard for me to refuse you."

Lillian kept glancing at the decanter and Henry filled her glass. They talked about Jennie, who would soon be a debutante and whom Henry would escort for the father-daughter dance at the Patriarchs' Ball at Delmonico's, and about her husband, who was in Rochester for a board meeting. Mrs. Underwood said that he treated her generously. The munificence had taken some getting used to, she confided, after Mr. Vanderburgh's illiberality. Illiberality of mind and pocket. She drank another sherry and she was getting drunk.

She declared, "You and I – only you and I – can discuss your father frankly. My selfishness revolts me, but your father's rectitude revolted me more. He was a pedant at heart. An exacting schoolmaster and a moral bookkeeper, tallying the ways we disappointed him."

She declared, "You can do anything if you have to. The truth is, I never loved anyone except my children. At least Jennie is safe now. But I'm worried about you. I fear you're too much alone."

She declared, "I only hope you can forgive me for what I've done."

She declared, "I have to go on living."

VI.

THE luncheon and a subsequent dinner two weeks later went well. By their third meeting, a cozy afternoon tea at Mrs. Underwood's house, they settled into their former ease with each other.

Caroline had returned to the city for a two month's stay with her parents. The Havemeyers – drawn into Lillian's web, Henry assumed; she must have spoken with them, although he doubted they needed much cajoling – invited them to an informal dinner at their Manhattan home and then, a few weeks later, to an afternoon of sleigh rides at their farm on Long Island. Henry and Caroline tried to ignore their hosts' bickering. They were invited to a Sunday musicale at Carley's brother's house as well, where they viewed H.O. and Louisine Havemeyer's superb art collection.

Henry studied a recent purchase, Monet's *Four Trees*, surprising Caroline with his absorption. A line of trees rose like long stalks, the thick purple bushes on the riverbank gathering like their skirts or tutus, as if the poplars were dancers frozen in time and space. He wished he could show the mysterious painting to Ida. It was Ida he wanted at his side.

But why not marry Caroline? Didn't he owe her that much?

Officially engaged, Henry and Caroline joined Lillian as they re-opened the property on Irving Place and inspected it. Of course, they would need to electrify it immediately. As Caroline rattled off the improvements she wanted to make, noting the various sales at Stern Brothers and the new Siegel-Cooper department store, and Lillian excitedly added her own suggestions, Henry's heart sank. Mr. Edison's incandescent lights would brighten this home and the next one, but these would still be houses of mourning.

The women were debating new curtains in the drawing room, lilac or chrysanthemum yellow. "What do you think, Henry?" Caroline asked.

Henry thought: It doesn't matter.

Henry thought: It's my own doing.

Henry thought: I wonder what my life would be like if I were marrying a woman I loved.

THIS SILENCE IS THE LARGEST I COULD FIND

It has no doors, no windows.
Yes, you may crawl inside it, but you must dig.
I don't know how long it will take.
What spade? Use your fingers, your toes.
Your teeth, if you have to. The soil
is bitter, don't swallow. Wait long enough
and you'll find silence sweet.
When good things finally come, which is
what true silence offers, you'll know
you are in. I mean, you'll find yourself
silent. You won't need any praise.
You won't need any people. You'll be
content you are there, alone, at the center
of silence, where the passage
of time and the passage of your one
real life are like details in a renaissance
painting. Where you watch a slow
barge being towed by a horse in a silent
movie and recognize your own
muddy thought. You'll see how infinitely
forgetful you are. How forgettable.
You'll watch a forest grow at the edge
of your silence, its roots anchored
in language. Each silent leaf,
an unspoken word. Each silent bird,
a song fluttering in your throat.

AND MILES TO GO BEFORE I SLEEP

(after Robert Frost)

Mother is nocturnal. Moments

of freedom come late into the evening.

After everyone has gone to bed,

she finds the strength, at 99, to rise

and roam—knowing or not knowing

remembering or not remembering

the times she's fallen, hit her head,

bruised her eye socket, but something

in her clouded mind pushes her to roam,

to spend hours between midnight

and sunrise searching as if lost in the woods—

no breadcrumbs to follow, no ravens to guide.

ICE

AFTER the snow came ice. It thickened itself around tree limbs, strangled telephone and cable wires so they drooped and sometimes snapped. Several houses around ours were consumed in darkness as the storm wore on. The golf course shut down, leaving me stranded at home with dad. I shivered from the cold but also from dreading days inside with him, alone together, without any means to escape.

He had his newspaper in-hand when I came down from my room, the paper itself wrapped in a thin glaze of ice. He unfolded it on the kitchen table, thawing it there while he brewed his coffee. I sat at the table and watched him pour coffee into his cup, breathe on it to cool it down, fill it with the requisite sugar and stir it together. The scent of it sickened me as it always did. Then he joined me at the table.

"What are you going to do now that you can't work?" He asked. "This would have been a fine time for you to have a hobby. Too bad you can't visit your boyfriend."

"He's not my boyfriend," I insisted. "I'll text him. I'll read a book. It'll be fine."

"We're damn lucky we still have electricity."

"What would we have done without it?" I asked, just to say something.

"What people always have done. Talk. Think. Create."

The heat kicked on with a loud murmur and it felt good coming out of the vents, initially cold but then warming up, steaming against the windows. I still shivered in my chair. I wasn't a coffee drinker but was tempted there, just to hold something hot in my hands that I could also pour into my body to warm it from the inside out.

Instead I stood up and picked up a banana, peeled it and ate it. I leaned against the counter by the sink. I wore jeans, a sweatshirt, a scarf and a knit cap even though I was indoors. Dad wore boots, corduroys with paint streaks all over them, a flannel shirt and his customary ball cap. He sipped his coffee loudly, continuing to blow on it, continuing to stir it as if just because he had nothing else to do. We were already bored and the ice had just fallen.

"I'm going out," I finally said.

"Out where?"

"Outside."

"It's a frigging frost farm out there," he said. "You'll freeze your fingers off."

"I'll bundle up. I'm just bored in here."

"You're bored everywhere," he said. "A typical teenager."

I ignored him, grabbed my parka, put it over me and then opened the front door to a blast of cold air that nearly knocked me off my feet. I steeled myself against it and walked outside. Everything was solid ice and there was something exquisitely beautiful about how the sun's muted light hit it. I knew I couldn't walk far if anywhere at all. My car was sealed in ice and besides, the streets weren't navigable at this point. Our small town didn't send salt trucks around often enough to make a dent in the ice, didn't pre-treat. So waiting was all we could do.

"Wait up," I heard dad say from behind me. "I'm coming with you."

I didn't want to wait. I wanted to run. But I held on and soon he came out too, equally bundled against the cold, his ball cap replaced by a stocking cap with the hood of a winter coat on over that. He breathed and it nearly froze in mid-air between us.

We took tentative steps onto the walk, everything crunching beneath our feet. I wished desperately for it not to be this way so that I could go to work as I always did and look at the vast expanse of greenery there, even though the trees were bare for winter and the grass was stunted. There were still golfers in winter, though not as many as in warmer months. They came and played while bundled up, they laughed and cursed and drank beer and it was all good.

Dad nearly took a tumble on the sidewalk and I had to grab his elbow with my gloved hand to steady him. "Watch your step," I said absently.

"I'm fine," he snapped back.

The odd thing was that he immediately headed to his car, a so-called luxury sedan that he drove hard but which had all-wheel drive unlike my little beater. He smashed the ice on the door handles with his fist. Somehow he pulled hard enough on the door that it opened for him with a huge crack of ice. Then he climbed in and started it. "Get in," he said to me as I stood there confused by what he was doing.

We pushed and pulled at the passenger door until it too gave way and I was able to enter. I sat inside and the heat of the car took a while to get going but once it did it flooded us. The windows gradually melted free of ice, starting with a small hole where the blower struck the glass and then the hole expanding to clear the windshield altogether. He turned the radio on first to a country station, which he apparently decided he didn't want, and then to a classical one, where he stayed, bobbing his head to the orchestral movements.

"Where are you planning to go?" I asked.

"Anywhere but here," he said, now tapping his fingers on the steering wheel.

I fought an urge to leave the car and return indoors. I was cold, still shivering despite the heater's efforts otherwise. But I hung on, like this was going to turn into something better, that maybe in the ice lay something concealed that we could unbury, something precious perhaps.

In time dad put the car into gear and rolled it back and forth as the ice made it difficult to gain traction. He finally was able to pull away from his spot and took to the street slowly, carefully, occasionally hitting a particularly icy spot that caused it to veer but he always turning the wheel to steer out of the slide. A person or two was out, some hacking at the ice with a scraper, others just standing and gawking in awe at the scene. We waved at them as we passed and they waved back.

I don't know why we didn't talk. It was like the ice held our tongues in its grip as well. Normally dad couldn't shut up, needling me with questions about my lack of a real job, my sexuality, my lack of direction. Now he seemed content to sway his head and arms in rhythm to the music, bathing in the heat, concentrating on the slow progress the car made on the icy streets. I liked him there in a way that I didn't when we were in the house together. This dad was calm, steady and serene. He seemed at last to have found a purpose that he otherwise lacked while stuffed in his living room chair with the TV on.

He finally turned the car into the golf course parking lot, which surprised me. He didn't golf and certainly couldn't have on this day anyway. He guided the car through the lot and up to the cart barn where he parked. No one was supposed to park there but then again no one was there to enforce the rule. The car idled and he turned the radio off.

"Why are we here?" I asked.

"I want to see where you work," he said.

"You never have before."

"Now I do, smartass."

"You picked a weird day to do it."

"Humor your father," he said. "Show me around."

He left the car running even as we stepped out. The course was a kingdom of ice now. Only a couple of birds made their way to the feeder to peck out suet. Otherwise the place was gripped in a stillness that reminded me of death. The chill in the air echoed that. We carefully stepped our way over to the door which I unlocked. We entered the office. The heat was on low there so I bumped it up a notch.

"Here we are," I said, still unsure what he was after.

"It's nothing much," he said, taking off his gloves and slapping them against the palm of his hand.

"I never said it was anything exceptional."

"And yet you spend a good portion of your life here like it is exceptional," he said.

"It pays my bills and lets me save."

"I guess that's something," he said. "Show me something else."

I shook my head, questioning his sanity at this point. But I opened the barn door to a new blast of cold air and we stepped inside it. All the carts were parked in their designated spots, plugged into chargers. A wren flew in the rafters. A scent of damp wood saturated the air. "This is where I spend the most time when I'm not outdoors," I said.

"It's cold in here. How can you stand it?"

"It's not always cold. Sometimes it's baking hot, like in summertime. It just depends."

"How relative of you," he said. "Show me something else."

"There's nothing else to see."

"What about the golf course, smartass?"

"It's impassable," I said.

"And you'll let that stop you? Christ, you kids today have no sense of adventure."

"We can walk it maybe."

"Then let's walk it."

We left the barn and trudged out through the icy pad and onto the course itself. Once we left pavement, it wasn't so hard to move. The ground gave a little, though not much, under our feet. But by the first tee I could see that he was wearing out. Normally he didn't exercise and this was a lot of walking for someone so otherwise sedentary. "We can rest here a minute if you like," I offered.

"Rest, hell," he said. "Let's keep moving."

So we kept moving, toward what I didn't know. We passed a pond that was sealed in ice. A crystallized sand trap. Flags flapped absently in the winds that blew through. As the course opened before us, the wind had nothing to slow it down and so it beat against our faces. Now I needed to rest. I located a bench between two holes and took a seat on it though it too was caked with ice and froze my ass there.

"Why are you stopping?" he asked.

"Because the wind's unbearable."

"Don't be a wimp. Keep moving."

"No," I said. "I'm stopping. If you want to be crazy, then you keep going."

He didn't protest anymore but sat down with me. We both shivered. "What are you looking for out here anyway?" I asked.

"Nothing. Maybe I just wanted to see what you do with your days."

"I keep an eye on things out here, that's all."

"And that satisfies you?"

"The money I earn satisfies me. The nature pleases me."

"It is pretty," he said. "Even now."

"You know, when the weather's nice we never walk together. Why are we doing it now?"

"Because I want to," he said. "I like winter. I like that everything's shut down for a day. I like that I didn't have to fight the morning rush hour to get to work today. I like that my bosses decided it was too treacherous. Screw them. They're wimps."

"Then the whole area's full of wimps," I said.

"It is. But you and I aren't going to be today. We're going to be strong and see the world frozen over." He grew animated as he spoke and even clapped a hand on my shoulder. I had never seen him like this.

"What's gotten into you?" I asked.

"Son, I'm bored. Things have been plodding along as they do, which is fine. But I don't always want to scan sales statistics on corn flakes. Sometimes I want to feel like the abominable snowman, primitive and wild, beat my chest and crush through the ice, you know?"

"I don't know, but I like that you're so excited right now."

"I know I'm hard on you most of the time," he said. "But just for today, let's be strong together. Let's be excited about something. Let's be intoxicated by the cold."

"This isn't going to last, you know."

"Life doesn't last. Your mother's memory is testament to that. So let's enjoy this while it's here."

I had fully decided that this crazy man couldn't be my father. My father sat in his chair and read his newspaper and harangued me day and night. This man seemed captivated by the world in a way that I had never seen in my father before. But I liked this man a lot. And for some reason, in all the excitement, I stopped shivering. The cold became irrelevant. What was relevant was that the ice hung on everything like mirrors, capturing the dim light of the sun and refracting it everywhere so that all seemed illuminated. The brightness very nearly blinded me, . And I loved it forthe hours that it lasted, even if we inevitably returned to our captivity.

THE CONSOLATIONS OF WATERLOO SUNSETS

This is a song about finding yourself alone and being okay with that.
This is a song about finding hope in endings.

[0:00 descending bassline]

ONE night in Washington, DC, my younger brother Joey fell on some subway tracks and died. He was alone, it was late, and it was the Fourth of July. It's why I hate the Fourth of July, and it's also, in a roundabout way, why I write. It's a common thing with sibling deaths, I'm told, to feel that you must carry the dead with you, that you started down a road together and you must continue down it together. When Joey died I felt this very strong need to live, like *really live*, with purpose and joy and whatever else I could muster, because I was living now for the both of us.

I rarely feel more alive than when I'm writing, so that became one of the ways I dealt with Joey's death. This is not an unusual way to grieve, but it is a funny way to *really live*, since the act of writing requires you to shut out the world and forget the self – at least, that's how it is when you're on a roll (writing is a little bit like sex in that way). So you could see writing as the opposite of living, as an escape from living, and my impulse to write through my grief as a desire to escape from a world where my brother no longer lived. Sometimes we write, sometimes we create our own little worlds in words, because we can't bear the world as it really is.

Escape or not, I needed to do it. First I wrote a sort of grief blog that I shared with friends and family. Then I pulled myself together and finished an academic book I'd been picking at for years. Then I wrote a few other things. Eventually, I wrote a book about the English rock band the Kinks, something well off my usual beat and probably the most satisfying thing I've written. I never would have tried it had it not been for Joey's life and death, so I dedicated it to him.

One of the chapters I wrote for that book was about the song "Waterloo Sunset." It talked about sunsets on the Thames and the inspiration artists have drawn from them. It also talked about death and rivers and smog and painters. It was a pretty good chapter and it took a lot of work, but it didn't fit with the other chapters – it was too personal, too much at odds with the detached intellectualism of the rest of the book – so I cut it. I have no idea how Joey felt about this song, and until recently it was never a particular favorite of mine, but while I was writing the book I became strangely attached to it.

One memory stands out. On a research trip to London I felt a very strong need to go to Waterloo Bridge and watch the sunset there, like this was what Joey would have done. So I went there on a bright June evening and listened to the song on my headphones and cried over Joey for the first time in years, not really in grief but in a kind of solidarity, like when you see someone at a funeral and you fall into their arms and sob together. That's what the song sounds like to me now: two people coming together in their loneliness and telling each other it will be okay. It's my song of consolation.

[0:08 one brother plays a looping lick on the electric guitar – it runs like a bridge over the other brother's strummed acoustic]

In the way of smart, introverted kids, Joey and I didn't open up much about the deep stuff. We'd be too embarrassed. But we did talk about music. If I was telling him about a new English band called Spoon that I really liked because they sounded serious at first but were actually quite funny, then I wasn't revealing anything deep about myself, except maybe I was. And when he was telling me that he already knew about Spoon and that they weren't from England but from Texas, then he wasn't revealing anything about himself, either, except that he liked it when I got things wrong.

We especially liked English bands (I'm certain I wouldn't have paid attention to Spoon if I'd known they were from Texas) and we liked English writers. We weren't queen-and-crumpet Anglophiles of the sort who buy checkout magazines about royal weddings. We liked a certain idea of Englishness that was eccentric and knowing and understated: not high-posh, more like mid-posh. Our adolescent tastes ran to Wallace and Gromit, Mr. Bean, Monty Python. When we were a bit older it was Richard Curtis and P. G. Wodehouse, Blur *and* Oasis, and Morrissey before he turned into a troll. A bit older still and Joey was gravitating toward Waugh while I took up Orwell. Joey was always a little snobbier than me and quicker to pronounce sweeping but lightly held judgments. I was always more of a class warrior, my own sweeping judgments informed more by Marx-and-Engels than by Oxford-between-the-wars.

If you imagine Evelyn Waugh and George Orwell rattling along a busy interstate in a battered Chevy Blazer somewhere between America's empty middle and its crowded east, sliding a Smiths CD out of a cracked jewel case and turning it up so the lyrics come in clear over the wind and engine roar, then you have the Doyle brothers in their mid-Oughts heyday. He's in a blazer and loafers and I'm in a hoodie and jeans. I need a haircut and he's just had one. We're muttering things in short bursts, at frequencies only audible, only ever really audible, to each other. We're thinking about where we'll get lunch. We're avoiding the important stuff.

[0:16 the vocals come in, a verse about a river and a crowd]

The Kinks were a brothers' band. Ray Davies wrote and sang most of the songs, and his younger brother Dave played lead guitar, the louder and fuzzier the better. The job of the other Kinks, who over the decades became a revolving cast of bassists and drummers and keyboardists, was to pave the road under Ray's words and Dave's electricity. They didn't have much in common, Ray and Dave, apart from being in the same band and growing up in the same family. Ray was detached and cerebral, an observer and a craftsman. Dave was young and flamboyant, still a teenager when the Kinks hit the big time, with a teenager's lusts and angsts and rages. While Ray stayed home writing songs and raising a family, Dave tore around the world doing drugs and causing trouble, and you could hear these dissimilarities in their music. The band's singles and albums were like a sonic graph of the slackening and tightening of the brothers' bond, a longitudinal study of two consciousnesses bound together by nothing but genes and history, sometimes clashing, sometimes diverging, sometimes merging. Out of that churn came some of English music's greatest songs.

Joey and I weren't quite like that. There wasn't a quiet one and a wild one: we were both the quiet ones, both Rays, with occasional streaks of Davelike excess. This sometimes made it difficult for us to talk but never difficult to understand one another. Like Ray and Dave – like all siblings, I suppose – we expressed our love through quarreling, sometimes quite violently (I once threw him through a window), but this ended when he grew bigger than me and I suddenly learned the art of placation. We also did the sibling thing of inventing our own secret worlds. If the Davies had their music, then the Doyles, at a much younger age, had their Pound Puppies, plush dolls who all had distinct biographies and habits of speech and lived in a world that looked like our bedrooms but was actually a kind of dog-centric amusement park. The closest we ever came to making music together was when we pretended these Pound Puppies were in a band: we'd turn on some music and move the Puppies around to make it look like they were singing and playing instruments. We even had an imaginary radio show, Pound Puppy Radio, that we recorded onto cassette tapes. The DJs were Pound Puppies, voiced by Joey and me, who improvised commentary and commercials between songs that we found on the radio or played on an adjacent tape deck. I listened to one of these tapes recently, one we made in 1987, when I was ten and he was six. It is not great entertainment – there's a reason they don't put puppet shows on the radio – but, for me, it's a very recognizable portrait of how we interacted at that age. It's mostly me talking and Joey laughing, the self-serious older brother providing the words and ideas while the younger one, divested of responsibility, made himself heard in whatever way he could. In this way, maybe we were a little like the Davies brothers.

I have a big pile of these tapes in a paper bag near my desk. If we had gone on to form a famous band, these tapes would doubtless have featured in the first ten minutes of the Netflix documentary about our career. As it is, they've moldered away in basements and attics for three decades, and so far I've only found the courage to listen to the one.

[0:35 the singer confesses he doesn't need friends – he's happy just watching the sunset]

When Ray Davies wrote "Waterloo Sunset" in 1967, he was afraid to show it to the rest of the band because it was too personal, because he thought it revealed too much of himself. Normally Ray wrote songs like a novelist writes dialogue, like a ventriloquist writes jokes. They weren't confessions, more like situations, observations about the world and its people that were sometimes written in the first person but rarely written as memoirs. Even when they were exploding with lust or rage, the songs were rarely transcriptions of Ray's own emotions. They were expressions of how an imagined narrator felt about things, or of how a different Ray, a Ray who wasn't the one singing the song, had once felt about things. On stage he never played himself. He played characters. He did funny voices and accents. He played the fool, the drunk, the spiv, the mod.

During the first period of their fame, in 1964 and 1965, the band acquired a rowdy, unwashed reputation, thanks largely to Dave's sound and fury. But by 1967, the time of "Waterloo Sunset," Ray was writing gentle story songs, social commentary songs, songs sung by characters who definitely weren't Ray. Any self-expression was indirect, incidental, tucked into corners.

"Waterloo Sunset" is one of those gentle story songs, but it doesn't have much of a narrative, and it doesn't have sharply drawn characters. There is only the haziest storyline: A distant observer watches millions of people swarming around Waterloo Station, on the south bank of the Thames. He's dazzled by the lights and dizzy with the crowds, but he feels no need to join them. He is happy in his cage, too lazy to go outside, a housebound Jimmy Stewart touched but untroubled by what he sees from his rear window. Amidst the swirl of the station, a boy named Terry meets a girl named Julie, just like every Friday night. They cross Waterloo Bridge wrapped up in each other, safe in their own little world, a distant mirror of the narrator's own contented solitude. And that's about it, a moment of grace amidst the city's bustle and swirl – until the very end, when the chord changes, the music swells, and you can almost hear the sun blazing out in a million colors before it drops behind the curve of the earth.

"Waterloo Sunset" has a swoony, dreamy quality that is unusual in a Kinks song. "It is effortless, making its small slam without a qualm." So wrote the architecture critic Ian Nairn in his London guidebook of 1966. He was speaking not about the song, which hadn't yet been written, but about Waterloo Bridge itself, and I think there is a sense in which the song sounds like the bridge. The opening bassline drops us into the scene from on high, giving way to Dave's delicate guitar licks that span the song like the arches of a bridge (Nairn again: "Five tense, shallow arches leap the Thames, drawing extra spring from hunched abutments ..."). Meanwhile, soft Beach Boys harmonies swell and fade like the tides of the Thames, lifting us above the madding crowd and into the misty heights from which the narrator watches the scene. Ray once said that he wanted the vocals to sound like a leaf falling through the air, and it has that quality, too. His frail voice could be blown away by the slightest musical breeze. "The song is about how innocence will prevail over adversity," he told the *Guardian* in 2016. "It starts out delicate, but by the end has become awesome in its power. Those triumphant chords come in – and the angels tell you everything is going to be OK." (Nairn: "The rhythm is syncopated further, because the arches don't run the full width of the bridge: there is a deep channel between them, which gives a breathtaking view from directly underneath, on the Embankment, looking down what seems to be a majestic colonnade.") But that moment of majesty is brief: the chords and the angels arrive only in the last few seconds, before a quick fade hurries you along your way. The moment may be tranquil, the underlying structure majestic, but it is also fleeting, like life.

So what, exactly, was Ray confessing here? Why was he embarrassed to show it to the others? You won't get a straight answer from Ray on this subject: over the years, he has said all sorts of things about "Waterloo Sunset," but not why it embarrassed him. He has said that it came to him in a dream and that he wrote it while hungover. He has said that it was originally called "Liverpool Sunset" and was about the "death of Merseybeat and all that," and that he had initially wanted to name the lovers Bernard and Dorothy. The names he settled on, Terry and Julie, could either refer (as he has sometimes said) to two of the most famous scenesters of Swinging London, Terrence Stamp and Julie Christie, who were filming *Far from the Madding Crowd* in Dorset at the time, or (as he has also said) they could be a nod to Ray's nephew and his girlfriend. He has said that he wrote the song for the generation who came of age before and during the Second World War, the generation of his six older sisters, working-class Londoners who were supposed to accept their lots in life and work in factories and things. In this way of listening to the song, crossing the bridge represents an escape from a life of drudgery into a more hopeful future, but it is someone else's future, not the singer's, that we're led to contemplate.

The reason the song has proved so durable, of course, is that it lends itself to all of these interpretations, or none. "It doesn't mean anything," Ray once admitted, "But when you hear the record, it means a lot." Sometimes a sunset just makes you want to sing, and you don't need a reason for it. Maybe that's what embarrassed him: he has allowed us to see him in an unguarded moment, he has allowed us to hear him singing in the shower, and he's worried about what we might think.

But once he shared the song with the band, "Waterloo Sunset" ceased to be a private moment and became the sound of a group. When we listen to the original recording, we're hearing not just Ray but the other Kinks, as well – Dave's guitar, Mick Avory's drums, Pete Quaife's bass – plus Ray's wife Rasa on backing vocals with Dave and Pete. When I listen to it, it's hard not to feel a little nostalgia on these strangers' behalf. They all sound so happy and harmonious. It's the backing vocals that do it. I don't know exactly how they recorded it, but I like to imagine Dave, Pete, and Rasa all gathered around a single microphone, shoulders touching, friends for now but not forever, wrapped in a moment that is simultaneously fleeting and eternal. The nostalgia comes because I know what they don't: that in two years Pete will leave the band, and that several years later Rasa will leave Ray, and that both endings will be awful. Even Mick will leave the Kinks before their run is through. Only the brothers will stick it out to the end.

[0:53 the sha la la chorus]

We were always going to be Kinks fans, Joey and I, although it took some time. I first found them through Van Halen's cover of "You Really Got Me," which got much more airplay on Oklahoma City radio during my childhood than the Kinks did. When I heard the originals, mostly early hits like "All Day and All of the Night" and "Tired of Waiting," they didn't grab me, probably because I wasn't yet a horny teenager. It wasn't until the mega-deluxe reissue of *The Kinks Are the Village Green Preservation Society* in 2004 that I realized there was more to the band than those early singles. At that time almost everything I knew about music came from the email newsletter of an uber-hip New York City record store, so when they praised the album as a great, little-heard masterpiece, I snatched it up. But even then I wasn't quite sold. The opening track's semi-sarcastic inventory of bygone Englishness tickled me right in my Anglophilia, but the rest of the album seemed uneven and difficult to unpack. So I shelved it and went back to my grad school rock: Arcade Fire, TV on the Radio, Sufjan Stevens, things like that.

I only really sat down and listened to the Kinks after Joey burned me a copy of a two-disc greatest hits collection. This was probably 2005 or 2006, when we were making CDs for each other to take on road trips between the east coast, where we lived, and Oklahoma, where our parents lived. I was fascinated by the way the band had evolved from those early, Van Haleny songs to the quirky story songs of the later Sixties. I usually stopped listening before the final overproduced singles of the Seventies and Eighties, but that was okay. I had what I needed, and I began to explore a little more.

Skip ahead to 2012, two years after Joey died, and I finally discovered the 1969 album *Arthur: Or, the Decline and Fall of the British Empire*. I found it thanks to a class I was teaching on twentieth-century Britain. Each class session was 85 minutes, which is a long time for anybody to listen to me talk, so I began inserting musical interludes about halfway through. Students who didn't rush off to the restrooms or vending machines got a short DJ set of songs from or about the era we were studying: Iron Maiden's "Passchendaele" or Motörhead's "1916" for World War One, Vera Lynn for World War Two, sprinklings of Noël Coward, any of a dozen songs wishing for the death of Margaret Thatcher. It was while I was compiling these sets that I found *Arthur*. The album was a soundtrack to an abortive television drama that Ray had written. It's about a depressed Englishman looking back on his life and contemplating his disappointing present, and it's full of songs about British history from the Victorian era to the Sixties, enough songs to fill nearly all of my musical interludes until we got to the Seventies. Somehow, I had never heard this album, and I began to think someone should use it as the basis for a novel. The liner notes, written by Ray's collaborator Julian Mitchell, gave a rough sketch of the narrative, and the songs conveyed the emotion – and really, what's a novel but narrative plus emotion? Then I decided that the person who should write that novel was me. Then I wrote the novel.

This is not something you're supposed to do when you're a full-time history professor at a regional comprehensive university with a young family and very little spare time. But after Joey died I'd promised myself that I would *really live*, and that meant working like hell to become a *real writer*, not just a writer of academic articles and monographs. So I wrote this thing because he had died, and also because he had lived, and while he lived he had cultivated in me not just an appreciation of the Kinks but a conviction that things like the Kinks and Englishness and music really mattered and were worth thinking deeply about.

That novel has never seen the light of day, which is probably for the best. But I did send out inquiries, and one publisher got back to me with an offer to write a different kind of Kinks book, the socio-literary-artistic history of the band that I finally published in 2020. I listened to an awful lot of Kinks during the two years it took to write this book, and I thought an awful lot about Joey. It was good to have something to do with my hands, good to have an excuse to pat and knead my grief, but it caused a curious inversion. The original idea was to write the book as a way of *really living*, but it turned out that when I was writing it, I wasn't living, but grieving. It was when I stopped writing for the day, when I put the computer and my grief to sleep, that I really did my living.

[1:15 second verse: Terry meets Julie on a Friday night]

"Waterloo Sunset" isn't really a grief song unless you squint your ears. If anything, it's a song that defies grief, the kind of song that catches a moment and saves it from the ashes. Ray once studied to be a painter, and he never quite lost the painter's knack of capturing a scene in all its shapes and angles. Sometimes he speaks of the song this way: "All the colours are there. I had to go into the studio and produce that record because that made up for me not being a painter. When I did the mix, I came down to Waterloo Bridge, to see if it worked. It was my substitute for not being able to paint it." Here, if we believe him, he was reversing the aspiration of those painters who have labored to make pictures that look like music – think of Whistler, think of Kandinsky – and mirroring Ornette Coleman's desire to make jazz that sounded like a Pollock painting. All art is about refusing death, I suppose, but to make music that sounds like a painting is especially daring because it's a refusal not just of death but of the temporality of music itself. Music, like life, has a beginning and end. A painting doesn't have those things, or, if it does, we measure them differently. How do you make something as effervescent as a song resemble something as persistent as a painting? How do you freeze time with sound?

A perhaps more answerable question: If "Waterloo Sunset" is like a painting, what kind of a painting is it like? Someone who knows their Thames sunsets might first imagine a refulgent yellow sunset by J. M. W. Turner. It's not a bad choice. Turner lived along the Thames all his life and painted it many times, sometimes at peace, and sometimes, as in his 1830s scenes of the burning of the Houses of Parliament, in majestic fury.

He had a skiff that he'd take onto the river to capture it at different times of day, but he liked the hour before sunset best. His sunsets are often apocalyptic, dwarfing humans and their petty creations in a piercing, divine brilliance. They are also melancholic. One of his most famous paintings, *The Fighting Temeraire*, depicts a wooden warship being towed down the river by a tugboat. The old campaigner is about to be broken up for scraps, its glory days forgotten in a belch of coal smoke, side-lit by a drooping, cloud-hooded sun. It is an image of the industrial age clearing away an outdated but perhaps more wholesome way of living, a warning about the future and a lament for a fading past.

You can't get much more Kinksian than that. This was exactly the sort of theme that was preoccupying Ray when he wrote "Waterloo Sunset," and it's all over *Village Green* and other albums from the period. Ray might have had *The Fighting Temeraire* in mind when he told an interviewer in 1994 that "Waterloo Sunset" was "about a world that was passing and we weren't appreciating. The underlying mood is very sad. The world will never be the same again and I'm a little bit scared but I take consolation in seeing the sunset and knowing that there will be another sunset and there will be sunsets long after I'm dead." He said something similar in his memoir, *X-Ray*, where he described standing on Waterloo Bridge as a teenager and watching the river flow "like blood flowing through a giant vein that led to the pumping heart of the Empire. I felt that there was a bigger tide coming that would completely flood the banks and submerge the Houses of Parliament. This was a tide of reality and change that was soon to turn England on its head."

A fiery apocalypse, a great city flooded, the inexorable rush of change – that's a lot of weight for a three-and-a-quarter-minute pop song to bear, and I'm not sure this one, tender and fragile as it is, is quite up it. So let's try this instead. A corpulent Frenchman in late-middle age, his dark moustache fading southward into a long white beard, eyes pinked by soot, stares at the Thames from the balcony of his suite in the Savoy Hotel. It is the very end of the nineteenth century, and London is the capital of the world. The sharp smell of burning coal is everywhere, but the river smells much sweeter than it once did, back when it served as both the principal sewer and the principal source of drinking water for the world's largest city. Now it is mainly the air that is slowly killing Londoners, a throat-clogging haze of carcinogens that is sometimes so thick that pedestrians crash into one another and church spires vanish into the heavens. "Fog everywhere," Charles Dickens had written on the first page of *Bleak House* in 1852, "Fog up the river, where it flows among green aits and meadows; fog down the river, where it rolls defiled among the tiers of shipping and the waterside pollutions of a great (and dirty) city. . . . Chance people on the bridges peeping over the parapets into a nether sky of fog, with fog all round them, as if they were up in a balloon, and hanging in the misty clouds." Decades later and the London fog has only gotten worse, but it is precisely this that has drawn the Frenchman here. He is fascinated by what the London fog does to the light above the Thames, and he has come to capture the river while it moves.

Claude Monet made roughly a hundred paintings of the Thames between 1899 at 1901, mostly from his balcony at the Savoy, at the northern end of Waterloo Bridge, although he also painted from St. Thomas' Hospital, across the river from Westminster. He painted the river in pale blue shadows cast by the arches of a bridge, obscured it with white clouds turning pink in a low-hanging sun, smeared it in a grey-blue haze emanating from the smoking chimneys on the south bank. He liked to do Charing Cross and Waterloo Bridges in the morning (he captured several Waterloo sunrises, but no Waterloo sunsets) and the Houses of Parliament at sunset, when the day's accumulation of smog made it look like a sea creature rising up through the mist. Monet once wrote that he loved London "only in winter with the fog, for without the fog London would not be a beautiful city." His London is mostly sky reflected in water, imposed upon but not unsettled by blurs of buildings and bridges. The London crowds are often in there, too, daubs of cream and blue who walk or ride near the river in ghostly procession, but they hardly matter to the play of light and color that's happening elsewhere. Monet's goal in these paintings was to suck viewers into a passing moment and leave them gaping there. He was painting in pursuit of what he called the *enveloppe*, the instant – no longer than, say, a popular song – when the light made the river appear just so, just before it became a different river. Alone on his balcony, he was trying to package the ephemeral and make it eternal.

Monet took a long time to finish these paintings. Like an obsessive musician doing take after take, he carried many of them back to his studio at Giverny and reworked them until they were just right. This fussing, I think, is how the paintings ended up with that chalky haze that makes them feel instantly nostalgic, like a faded photograph or a memory half-recalled. "Waterloo Sunset" has that quality, too, both because of the gauzy backing vocals and because the recording equipment they were using makes it sound so much of its time. It makes us think not so much about a scene present before us as of a scene as it once was, a river lit by memory. For that reason it sounds more like a Monet than a Turner to me, more like a delicate dance in the fog than a careening spectacle lit by fire.

[1:52 those sha la las again]

When he wrote "Waterloo Sunset," Ray Davies had plenty of his own memories of the Thames to draw on. He remembered visiting the Festival of Britain on the south bank in the summer of 1951, with its huge, cigar-shaped Skylon Tower that looked, at the time, like the future. He remembered spending some nights at St. Thomas' Hospital on the Thames at the age of thirteen, when a serious injury required him to get a tracheotomy. The procedure nearly killed him, and during his recovery the nurses wheeled him onto the balcony to look across the river toward Westminster – the same view Monet had – and out toward Waterloo on the right. He remembered changing trains at Waterloo Station on his way to art college a few years later, and, later still, he remembered courting Rasa along the Embankment and planning their future together. Waterloo Bridge, the station, the south bank, the Thames – that area, he once told Jon Savage, was his "center."

For the previous generation, the generation of the Davies sisters, the area held its own romantic memories. This was partly thanks to a 1930 play by Robert Sherwood called *Waterloo Bridge* and three subsequent film adaptations, all of which were about love and separation on or near the river. In the play, a man and a woman meet on Waterloo Bridge during World War One. The woman is a prostitute, the man a soldier, and the drama revolves around their blossoming relationship and the woman's efforts to keep her profession hidden from him. The most successful film adaptation was the 1940 version starring Vivien Leigh and Robert Taylor. In this version, the man and the woman (now a ballerina) meet on the bridge and become lovers. The man is called up to the front and subsequently reported dead. The woman falls into despair and resorts to prostitution. When the man returns to London alive, the woman tries and fails to keep her recent past from him, ultimately committing suicide by throwing herself under a truck on Waterloo Bridge.

It's a grimly appropriate ending. Today the guides on London sightseeing boats will tell you that Waterloo Bridge is known as the Ladies' Bridge because of the women who helped construct the current bridge during World War Two. I'm not sure how many people other than tour guides ever call it that, but I do know that some Londoners knew the old bridge, the one built in 1817, as the Bridge of Sighs because of all of the suicides that happened there – and because it was the title of an 1844 poem by Thomas Hood about a seduced and abandoned woman who prefers death to dishonor and throws herself from the bridge, "Perishing gloomily / Spurr'd by contumely." The poem became so popular that many of the paintings and illustrations you'll find of the old bridge feature wretched women preparing to jump from it, or falling from it, or lying dead beneath its wide arches. "This is where it is," a toll-keeper told Charles Dickens one night in 1853, "if people jump off straight forwards from the middle of the parapet of the bays of the bridge, they are seldom killed by drowning, but are smashed, poor things; that's what they are; they dash themselves upon the buttress of the bridge."

But this wasn't just a Victorian thing. In 1910 the poet Douglas Goldring imagined the archetypal scene of a "pale girl" contemplating suicide just at sunset, "where the West is olive-pink / And rosy mists the river shade" above a Thames that is "sullen, purposeful and strange" running beneath a "patient bridge that will not change." Here sunset represents not hope but hopelessness, a full stop after which "will come no night, no dream." In 1923 Noël Coward opened his revue *London Calling* with a woman being notified of her husband's suicide off Waterloo Bridge: "Yes, the one next to Charing Cross, —No, no, no, that's Blackfriars. Don't be so silly, Flossie, you know perfectly well Westminster comes first, then— the one with trains on it, then Waterloo." In this tradition the Thames is not just a dirty old river but the River Styx, a passageway between life and the afterlife. Or maybe it's the River Lethe, the river of forgetfulness from whose waters the dead drink to forget their past lives.

But the Thames isn't a river of forgetfulness, not really. It's a river of memories, more memories than you can count, even if you're just counting up the times it's appeared in the works of writers and painters and musicians, even if you're just counting up the sunsets. Each time we encounter one of these little memories it shapes and reflects and absorbs our own. "Remembrance! as we glide along," sang Wordsworth of a sunset on the river at Richmond in 1798:

> Such views the youthful bard allure,
> But, heedless of the following gloom,
> He deems their colours shall endure
> 'Till peace go with him to the tomb.
> —And let him nurse his fond deceit,
> And what if he must die in sorrow!
> Who would not cherish dreams so sweet,
> Though grief and pain may come to-morrow?

The poet here is floating westward down the Thames, toward the sun, oblivious to the gloom that's shadowing him from behind, and Wordsworth wants to keep it that way: let him have his momentary paradise, let him have his singing. In *Daniel Deronda* (1876), George Eliot sends her hero out rowing and singing upon the Thames in a similar sunset reverie. Daniel is adrift in his life, just back from a spell abroad and wondering whether to join battle with the world. In his solitude he absently sings some lines from Dante that are usually translated as, "There is no greater pain than to remember a happy time when one is in misery." He sees a young woman: she is dipping her woolen cloak in the water to make a drowning shroud out of it. Daniel's song has penetrated her, seeming to endorse what she's about to do. But Daniel rushes over and rescues her, and a major plotline is set in motion.

Other writers have dwelt in the gloom. Conrad opened that most river-obsessed of stories, *Heart of Darkness*, the Thames at sunset, just as "the sun sank low, and from glowing white changed to a dull red without rays and without heat, as if about to go out suddenly, stricken to death by the touch of that gloom brooding over a crowd of men." Dickens opened *Our Mutual Friend* on an equally sinister note, with a man and his daughter searching the Thames for corpses as "a slant of light from the setting sun glanced into the bottom of the boat, and, touching a rotten stain there which bore some resemblance to the outline of a muffled human form, coloured it as though with diluted blood." Then there's Dr. Seward in Bram Stoker's *Dracula*, stepping away from his grim asylum to find cold comfort in a Thames sunset, "with its lurid lights and inky shadows and all the marvelous tints that come on foul clouds even as on foul water." There isn't much consolation in these scenes, more like an undertow of dread, but, that, too, is a perfectly reasonable way to feel about a river.

[2:14 third verse: Terry and Julie cross the river, safe and sound]

Joey and I had no shared memories of London – when we went there, we went separately. But we did share stories. The last time he was there he spent most of his time with an Oklahoma friend who had somehow ended up addicted to heroin in a squat in Tower Hamlets. While the friend was out scoring, Joey wrote postcards and went bookshop-hopping. Then he wrote me a long email with travel tips. He told me about a chocolate shop in Spitalfields that was started by some disillusioned lawyers after they visited South America. He told me about the pub he was writing in, which had a large collection of country music and Faces LPs. He told me about a bookshop in Notting Hill where an old man in tweed was complaining loudly about how long novels are. Then he told me about the first time he was in Notting Hill. It was a high school trip some years earlier, and he had been delighted to see that the cinema in Notting Hill was playing the movie *Notting Hill*. He was tempted to go see it – he found Hugh Grant charming and coincidences comforting – but instead he and some friends got a bottle of vodka and drank it on the roof of their hotel.

He wrote me that email one January while I was in London working on a book about the British Empire. I was alone, and he was trying to make me feel less so. But I didn't really mind the solitude. My chief memories of that time are of wandering alone through the city at every spare moment, particularly at night, and glorying in the solitude. After a day at the National Archives in Kew, I would pack up my notes and take the Tube to a station in central London. After grabbing something to eat, I would wander for hours practicing night photography with my new digital camera, often balancing the camera on bollards or rubbish bins to minimize vibrations. I snapped crowds hustling down Villiers Street, ice skaters at Somerset House, cheesemongers in Borough Market, the lights of Hammersmith Bridge. They were solitary, these night walks, but not lonely. I felt that lovely freedom you get in a foreign city where you run no risk of running into somebody you know. My attention was rapt, my senses primed, my path eccentric. I needed no friends: the city was mine.

I suspect this is how another American in London, James McNeill Whistler, felt when he painted his series of nocturnes along the Thames in the 1860s and 1870s. He nearly said as much in a lecture in 1885:

> And when the evening mist clothes the riverside in poetry, as with a veil, and the poor buildings lose themselves in the dim sky, and the tall chimneys become campanili, and the warehouses are palaces in the night, and the whole city hangs in the heavens, and fairy-land is before us – then the wayfarer hastens home; the working man and the cultured one, the wise man and the one of pleasure, cease to understand, as they have ceased to see, and Nature, who, for once, has sung in tune, sings her exquisite song to the artist alone.

Whistler liked to observe the Thames at night – atop a bridge, aboard a rowboat, on a balcony at the Savoy (it was he who recommended the hotel to Monet) – and, after observing it, he would withdraw to paint it from sketches or memory. What he was after was a sound as much as a scene: he was one of those painters who approached his work like a musician, arranging tone and form to bring order out of chaos. The term he chose to describe these paintings, "nocturnes," is a musical term, as were many of the titles he chose: *Symphony in White, Harmony in Blue and Gold, Arrangement in Grey and Black.* They aren't pop songs, these nocturnes – they're too cool and abstract for that – but they can give you the same feeling as a pop song.

Which brings me back to "Waterloo Sunset." I said earlier that the song is like a Monet, but it is also like a Whistler – or maybe it's better to say that Whistler's nocturnes are like sleepy cover versions of the song. They have the same colors, the same tones: blues and violets, greys and flashing yellows, solitude, peace, a quiet awe. Often in Whistler's paintings there is just one person visible – a solitary bargeman, a figure standing at the river's edge – with maybe a few other people up on a bridge. All are painted with the same colors as the river or the sky or the land. The paintings depict solitude but not loneliness, because how can you be lonely when you're made of the same stuff as the landscape? The painter is there too, of course, watching the figures from a bridge or a balcony or a boat, just like the narrator who watches Terry and Julie from his window. The figures we see may think they're alone, but they're not. There's Whistler with his sketchbook, Ray with his piano, me with my camera, catching and holding them before they're gone.

[2:50 the looping electric lick returns, one brother carrying the other over the river]

The last time I was in London was in the summer of 2018, eight years after Joey died, when I was working on my Kinks book. I stayed in Muswell Hill for a couple of nights, photographing the places where the Davies brothers had passed their youth and wondering how the place might have changed. Then I moved to a student room at the London School of Economics for a few nights while I scouted locations for a summer course I thought I'd teach. I took a Rock 'n' Roll Walking Tour around Soho, visited the house in Mayfair where G. F. Handel and Jimi Hendrix once lived (not together), photographed a Battersea housing estate, and, one afternoon, headed out to Twickenham to visit the Eel Pie Island Museum, which commemorates a bygone dance club in the middle of the Thames that once hosted acts like the Rolling Stones, the Small Faces, Bowie, and the Who (but not, as the chap at the museum told me, the Kinks). None of these places made me think of Joey, particularly, which was strange. I often feel closer to him when I'm travelling, especially when I'm travelling alone, but on this trip I was so preoccupied with other things that I didn't give a thought to his rooftop vodka parties or his cranky old men in bookshops. I could have used this trip as an occasion to visit once more all the places he had told me about, to imagine him standing beside me as I sampled some lawyer chocolate or flipped through some LPs in a Tower Hamlets pub, but the thought didn't even cross my mind.

Because it had been eight years, because the grief had been so fully absorbed into my bloodstream that it had altered my chemical composition. I didn't feel like I needed to do anything with the grief, because it wasn't outside of me: it wasn't something I enacted, but something that I was. But then I had a thought. While I was walking along the Thames path in Twickenham, after Eel Pie Island, I decided to try catching the sunset on Waterloo Bridge. It was getting late, and it was a long way to central London, but I thought I could probably make it. It had been a metallic June day, blue and clear, so the sunset wouldn't be much, neither a Turner nor a Monet (and I'd have to wait until full darkness for a Whistler), but the rest of my evenings were booked and this would be my only chance. I checked the sunset time on my phone, estimated my route and speed, and decided that if the District Line wasn't too slow I could rendezvous with the sun before it vanished. I said earlier that Joey found coincidences comforting. He also liked to force coincidences, by, say, putting on the Eagles song where they mention Winslow, Arizona, at the very moment he'd be driving through through Winslow, Arizona. My idea was that I'd get to Waterloo Bridge just at sunset and play the song on my headphones while I watched the sun slip into the river. It was a corny kind of joke, but I thought he'd get it.

[2:58 the chord changes, and the angels come in]

The train took longer than I'd expected. As I rushed along the

Embankment toward the bridge, past Cleopatra's Needle, past the faux-Parisian posterior of the Savoy, I rehearsed the line from the *Muppet Movie* that I use as an aide de memoire for keeping track of sunsets. Fozzie and Kermit are on a cross-country trip and joyfully lost. They're singing about their wrong-turnings and mishaps and at one point Fozzie says, "Hey, I've never seen the sun come up in the west!" This movie was a fixture of my and Joey's childhood, and that line is how I learned – and how I still remember – that the sun sets in the west, but it doesn't rise there. I was now heading northeast, so I knew that the sun would be behind me. I couldn't see it from where I was on the Embankment, but perhaps once I was up on the bridge...

But no. The sky was still blue, scored by jet trails and marbled with dark and light clouds, and the sun was obviously still above the horizon, but I couldn't see it for the trees and buildings. I put on my headphones anyway, put on "Waterloo Sunset," and walked toward the south bank. The bridge was nearly empty, but even if it had been swarming with people I'd have felt alone. I know I've said that grief didn't stalk me on this trip, but while I was racing there I think I had this idea that I'd meet Joey at the bridge, that I'd find some kind of sign or feeling, some thinness between his world and mine. I'm always feeling around for things like that, and sometimes I find them, even if I have to strain a bit. But this was just a bridge, a fairly unremarkable concrete bridge when you're actually up on it, with white metal railings and bike lanes and bus lanes and grey, wet-looking smudges on the stone.

When the song finished I played it again: one brother up high with the top notes, the other brother down below, hard to hear, strumming the acoustic. A bridge and a river, two lovers, the world through a pane of glass. I looked to my left, to the east, where I knew that there would be no sun. But I was wrong, because suddenly there it was. A glass building near Saint Paul's Cathedral, some anonymous office building that people of an artistic temperament probably hate, was glowing orange like it was on fire. It had caught the light of the sun from across the river and was reflecting it back at me: a sunset in the east instead of the west. It was a joke so good it brought tears to my eyes.

SHARING THE WOUND

I like it here, beyond signposts
and summaries, says the painter Clyfford Still
to a friend who's moving to the hill country "forever."
Yes, says Still, we all should disappear
into what we must do.

For my part, I travel, often alone,
as you note, into a wounded opening on canvas
to enter the crater, explore its cause,
how I've been altered, to greet the color
of healing that happens through welcomed exposure.

Among the orchards of the farm where you'll work,
what awaits inhabiting? I no longer care much for labels.
We enter our endeavors to learn.
Let's call this one: "1944-N No. 2."

Farewell, my friend, for you and I
are like two seekers pausing
at the river to dive into the rushing
and parting with the same shared stuff.

ÉDOUARD VUILLARD AND A LITTLE GIRL WITH A HOOP

Dear woodsy girl with wind-shaken pond eyes
under a canopy thick with birth and after-birth
and floral pink rampant on the earth, you burst
to skip with your shoulder-high hoop, yet freeze
as you spot me out here in my artist's get up.

Behind, your family forages for chestnuts
under heavy branches. I have not come to snatch them
which you guess
from how I dress.
Rather I'm gathering
images, arrested by light
across your kin's bent and stooped backs
as pink flames through trees, fattens around florid azaleas.

We stare at each other. Silence narrows us.
Your eyes widen. Words catch in my throat.
Back to spinning your hoop in a blue smock, you're off
forgetting me who did not elbow anyone for a fresh chestnut
loose and fallen from some cracked-open bag

PHOTO OF FATHER ON A MOTORCYCLE

Looking like a Beatle: bowled hair thick and sideswept.
Corner of sun catching cattails, swinging to a silent tune,
bike draped in sugar crystals—glazed leather seats, white
stripes bleached and my daddy's face nuzzled in his collar,

my daddy's eyes windows to his Oldies soul, gleamy
the way eyes get after hearing songs you used to love—
little darlin', it's felt like years since it's been here…As a kid,
I barely heard my daddy play guitar. He'd hide in his room

plucking strings patiently, murmuring words to "Landslide,"
"Werewolves of London," "Here Comes the Sun,"
would bow his head and sway like those cattails or a grooving
turtle, some notes missed or dawdling under his fingers

while he hummed in his quiet studio
and I stood outside his door, listening.

GOOD PEOPLE

Tell me if the star-shaped mole is cancerous. If I'll be the statistic
improbability. Remind me: how does the medicine work if it ate
my grandfather's face? He always healed too quickly

and hurt again. Show me the bruises on my grandmother's chest
after he beat her in the bedroom. Tell me how she hid them
from her children. Then show me my mother's breasts,

where her cancer rooted. Tell me who's going to die
first: my mother, my father, my brother, or me. How do I stop
being fatalistic? Promise me: I'm not good enough

to die young. I'm always begging to become a bad person.
Should I be this scared of dying if I don't believe in God? Why
don't you tell me if I believe in God? I want to know

what my grandmother saw as she slipped away in hospice;
how machines keep us alive. Why do I always remember
my father with a bowed head? When I, as a child, pointed

to each corner of my bed, promising my mother
there were good people there—was I trying to protect us?
Did something once protect us?

MVMOMS

On my last trip to the Washburn branch of the Hennepin County Library as a volunteer book reviewer, I elbow the automatic door opener. I am oblivious that, before my next visit, I will resign my unpaid position in order to preserve my punctuational integrity. When the heavy door swings open, I squeeze my blue nylon double stroller through the entrance.

"Say hi to the librarian!" I instruct my stroller passengers. Gloria, the librarian, smiles at us from behind the front desk. My four-year-old twins wave at her with the tempered enthusiasm of a Midwestern dairy princess on a bedazzled truck bed in a small town parade.

I steer their unwieldy chariot toward the children's section, past a row of computers outfitted with child-sized headphone sets and colorful keyboards, past an appealing graphic novel display, then through the moody teen bookshelves. My twins grab at the outward facing hardcovers, all of which feature unhappy adolescents tilting their heads beneath edgy, graffiti-style titles. We emerge from our wheeled journey through the stacks to a communal play area under a vibrant ceiling mural.

"Here we are!" I unbuckle my twins from their stroller restraints. They slide down from their fabric seats and beeline to the toys. The children's librarian calls this the pre-literacy section, but a label like pre-influenza or pre-RSV or pre-strep fits, too.

"I'm going to look for books," I say, and scoot over to the picture book bins. My kids know their way around. We visit the library often, a least once a week, to exchange books, attend storytime, or just to kill time at a free destination that welcomes us and our germs before we pick up my oldest son, the twins' big brother, from his morning preschool program.

Today, our library visit has a purpose: I need to find three books on a theme. Or find three books that I like, then fabricate a theme that ties them together. I write book reviews for a parent newsletter and my monthly column is due by the week's end.

Randomly, I start with a book bin labeled C, but it contains only books authored by Eric Carle. Not helpful. Every literate parent already knows of Carle's ridiculous, binge-eating caterpillar. And they most likely know Carle's next most popular book, Brown Bear, Brown Bear, What Do You See? and his third most popular book, the derivative Polar Bear, Polar Bear, What Do You Hear?, both of which feature a preposterous premise. In each book, beautifully illustrated animals spy or eavesdrop on other creatures which, in a real world environment, they would flee from or eat. Eric Carle doesn't need my recommendation.

I glance at the D and E books. At the front of the F bin rests Thank You, Bear by Greg E. Foley. That's a cute one. Less well known. Its titular character finds a perfect present for his best friend and, on the way to gifting it, a whole forest of creatures tries to talk the bear out of giving it away. The theme "Stay true to yourself" comes to mind. So does "Don't give a shit about what woodland critters think." Then I arrive at a simpler, less profane theme: "Bears." Brilliant. What is the deal with bears in kids' literature, I wonder? Stories about huge and sometimes-predatory mammals must trace back to myths from pre-industrial times, when dangers emerged from the wilderness. Not like now, when most dangers emerge from too much taming, now that humans have demolished and polluted and raised the temperature of Earth's remaining wilderness areas. I make a mental note for next month's theme, maybe climate change, severe weather, or mass extinction.

Have I done bears before? I think back. I can remember months where I've compiled a set of books on themes of space exploration, the alphabet, naughty protagonists, alternative fairy tales, winter, colors, and instructive bunnies. But I haven't done bears. For now, I'm on to something. I have a tentative theme and one book, which halfway completes my library mission.

I check on my twins. They pile fake fruit into woven baskets, then transfer their harvest from a wooden Melissa and Doug structure over to an aggressively cushioned window seat that wraps around the entire, circular play area. This activity exercises all of their pre-literacy skills, plus probably exposes their immune systems to a light staph infection or Herpes simplex virus.

They sit down and pretend to share a plastic peach.

"Not in your mouth!" I chastise.

I appreciate the library's family-friendly design. Before I had kids, I aspired to work at a library like this one, but over in the grown-up section, which is hushed and serious. I wanted to uphold the principles of democracy by offering unfettered access to a wide array of viewpoints in reading material and other media. And if not that, then I wanted to answer reference questions on complex topics. Or, at least, help library patrons with important business, such as refilling printer toner and converting .doc files to .pdfs. I still, wistfully, hope that someday I will get to share one of my life's true passions: exporting citations from electronic research databases into properly formatted works cited pages. Modern Language Association rules for works cited pages are my favorite. But, as a true style guide-head, I'm equally proficient in APA rules for reference lists, as well as Chicago and Turabian rules for bibliographies.

Is there anything better in this world than definitive rules about punctuation in style guides that take a hardline on whether periods belong inside or outside a set of parenthesis identifying publication year? That stipulate a singular, lowercase p to identify a singular page number, and a douple pp to identify a range of page numbers? Rules for whether to initial or spell out an author's first name? I take pleasure in a perfectly formatted bibliography like some people take pleasure in a pressed crease in their dress pants. Or a ROYGBV-ed pantry shelf. Or artfully swooshed whipped cream on a perfectly plated dessert. I am not persnickety about pants or plates or pantry shelves, but I recognize that obsession with detail. Like the Radiohead song, Everything in Its Right Place, which Thom Yorke very well could have written to express his enthusiasm for rules about one-inch page margins.

I realize that my style guide dream vocation is more of an academic writing center-type of job than a public library-type of job. I narrowly missed my calling when I went to graduate school for library science instead of a writing program. But I (mistakenly) thought that library science was a practical career with many exciting job opportunities. I couldn't justify the time and expense of a frivolous writing degree, so I chose a profession where, at least, I could be surrounded by books.

My preference for following citation rules over answering reference questions doesn't matter, anyway. I never realized my public library career dream. After I earned my master's in library science, the only jobs I could land were at a shoddy business library, and then an online for-profit college (think: the University of Phoenix, but less notorious). I don't get paid to punctuate or answer anything now. When my twins were born just five years into my librarian career, I quit my job to stay home and care for them, trading database searches and pdf conversion lessons for full-time parenting.

Earlier I wrote "parent newsletter," a phrase that sounds legitimate, nearly sophisticated, but it's not accurate. I only wrote "parent newsletter" because the actual organization that distributes my volunteer book review column sounds so hokey that I can barely type it. The newsletter isn't actually for parents, in general. It's for moms, specifically. Moms like myself who belong to a club called Minnesota Valley Mothers of Multiples. Mothers of Multiples, as in moms of twins, triplets, and rare higher order multiples like quadruplets or quintuplets. MVMOM for short.

When I was pregnant with my twins, I joined the group in order to gain early shopping privileges at a twice annual event where members sell outgrown baby clothes and gear in a giant suburban high school gymnasium. But at the sale, I observed that the volunteer workers looked friendly and fun. So, after my twins were born, I attended my first MVMOM monthly meeting on a mini-quest to find mom friends. I left my home in Minneapolis and drove several miles south on highway 77, past the Mall of America, and across a big bridge that spanned the Minnesota River. I ate snacks, chatted with other MVMOMs, listened to a guest speaker, and drove home.

At another MVMOM event, a playdate at an indoor playground, I looked around and noticed that every other woman there, aged 25-55, wore the same outfit—chunky wool sweater or a fleece jacket, cross body canvas bag, and Sorel snow boots—and was engaged in a high stakes negotiation with a toddler or two over whether or not to eat the cookie now or save it for later. And I thought, yes, here I am, and there I am, and over there I see several versions of me, too. I looked the part, like a movie extra in the background, mouthing fake dialogue. But, it turned out, I just blended in with the MVMOMs. I didn't feel like I fit in.

I didn't fit in because I was embarrassed about my unemployment. The MVMOMs seemed, on a whole, okay with stay-at-home life. Some of them probably chose it on purpose. And I, an asshole, clung to the second wave feminism float I was raised on, and avoided calling myself a stay-at-home mom. When my twins were infants, I thought I'd be jobless just until all three of my kids hit a more affordable daycare center pricing level. Working full time just didn't make sense, not when childcare totalled more than the take-home pay I earned as a reference librarian. I never lied about having a job, but I hated to admit that I didn't work. Even at MVMOM meetings, which were the absolute safest spaces to talk about my fragile, sleep-deprived baby brain and my sensitive, hormone-charged feelings. My reticence to socialize as my authentic self meant that I never quite gelled with anyone.

Besides, logistics made it hard for me to get to a lot of the in-person meetings and activities organized for the benefit of moms with babies the age of mine. The drive to the suburbs south of the Minnesota River consumed too much time. My twins didn't like to nap concurrently. My preschooler had a very part-time school schedule. My husband worked long office hours and frequently traveled for his job, leaving me with the bulk of the housework and childcare.

I also felt that there was a sensibility difference I could never quite achieve. This, too, was wrapped up in the weighted blanket of misogyny that trapped me in my discomfort with maternal unemployment. Sometimes people make a distinction between different types of intelligence: street smarts and book smarts, especially when they want to take a grade grubber down a peg. I'd add a third category: suburb smart. The MVMOMs were suburb smart; they had this way of assessing a situation, then making it safer, more comfortable, and inclusive. Hanging out with MVMOMs was like living in a life hack content social media channel. I marveled at how they knew to fill a restaurant-size sheet pan with ice upon which to place salads for potluck picnics. And how they always chose parks with fenced-in playgrounds for playdates. From the MVMOMs I learned to bring small Ziplock baggies to movie theaters for easy popcorn splitting; that a shrunken blazer instantly classes up any outfit, even yoga pant or pajama leggings; that Rice Krispie Treats, in a pinch, count as a nutritionally sound breakfast. The MVMOMs cleaned up after events with an ethic that surpassed the most diligent Leave No Trace wilderness campers. They set up meal trains for bed resting club members with scheduling precision that rivaled efficiency experts. They built up the confidence of flailing members faster and more effectively than a daytime talk show host and an ultra-caffeinated studio audience. I am not suburb smart. I'm inclined to wallow in hardship.

Even though I didn't feel like I fit in, I loved the MVMOMs. They were the first people to congratulate me on the birth of my twins without adding any qualifiers. They didn't gasp or shout "Wow!" or ask invasive questions about natural birth or fertility treatments. They were the only ones in my whole life who understood the particularities of parenting twin infants, both the challenges and the joys. How hungry breastfeeding two babies, simultaneously, made me. How no one in my house ever got enough attention. How, not too long after the worst of the round-the-clock feeding and diapering and sleeping or trying to sleep pit of infant parenting, I felt overwhelmed with good fortune.

Even though I was a tertiary member, I had a very keen desire to be a part of MVMOM, to contribute in some way. Volunteers ran the club, from leaders like President and Sale Coordinator, to workhorses like New Member Greeter, and Guest Speaker Booker. None of the roles seemed achievable for me because of the distance, my husband's work schedule, my lack of suburb skills, and my preoccupation with stay-at-home mom identity denial. Except, there was a volunteer newsletter editor who sent out a monthly bulletin with articles and blurbs that I enjoyed reading. After several months of seeing messages from the newsletter editor appealing to members for content, I thought to myself: I could write about kids' books! So I pitched a little book recommendation column that the volunteer newsletter editor immediately accepted.

Writing brief reviews of three books every month made me feel like a legitimate MVMOM member, a contributor to the community, even though my participation was asynchronous and online. Plus, I enjoyed the autonomy. Except for the newsletter editor's deadline, nobody told me how to write the reviews. I picked the books, evaluated them, and distilled their best qualities into brief, three- to four-sentence paragraphs. Every month I turned in perfect copy that the newsletter editor pasted into her newsletter template.

To curate my bear theme, I flip through more bins and grab each picture book with a bear on the cover to check out and evaluate at home. I don't have a rubric, just an innate method for evaluating books. I recommend books that I enjoy enough to pay attention to while I read to my kids. Most books make me zone out while reading because they're not engaging. Mediocre books make my voice go monotone and my mind wander. My kids don't seem to notice when this happens, and if they notice, they don't care that I read to them in my mom-zombie voice. Good read-aloud children's books hold my attention and make me read with expression. I recommend books with clever language, endearing characters, tight plots, and captivating artwork.

My twins abandon the toy fruit and help themselves to books from the pile I stack on the cushioned window seat. They engage in what the children's librarian calls pre-reading: flipping pages, studying illustrations, and making plot inferences. It's a great source of pride for me that, in addition to alphabet letters, they also know ? and ! The three of us sit on the floor for a few minutes, a rare moment of calm and inaction.

My twins and I swivel our heads when we hear a small voice cry out, "Why?!"

"Because I said, 'we can only check out two books,'" the child's adult— mom, nanny, grandma; I can't tell—raises her voice, too.

I want to speak up in defense of the other child, the would-be bookworm on the other side of the children's area, who crescendos a righteous protest against his adult's paltry two-book limit. I want to correct the adult. The limit is actually fifty books per library card, but I refrain from interfering. Instead, I let my twins take turns swiping our big bear book stack through the automatic checkout machine and layering them on the undercarriage of our stroller.

It bothers me when I overhear parents deny their children certain genres, like graphic novels or comics, or types of media, like books on compact disc. Or denigrate Garfield. Or put an arbitrary maximum on books to check out. For my household, we've already had to get a card in my oldest son's name because, between the three kids and I, we can easily exceed my card's fifty-book limit. I love to feel morally superior by not imposing any literary limits on my kids. Probably this is what it feels like to be unabashedly sex positive, or to have lived through the 1990s without acquiring food issues. I wouldn't know; I'm a prudish body dysmorphic. The library is the one place I feel smugly liberated.

On the walk from the library to my older son's preschool, I try to think up all of the books I've recommended to the MVMOMs over the last two and a half years, since I started my column. Exotic pets in bathtubs. Picture books by literary figures: bell hooks, Margaret Atwood, and, of all the 20th century poetry monsters, Ted Hughes. Scary books. Counting books. Books on lions. Books on death: a column I worked on after my mother-in-law died, and in response to a regular question on the MVMOM message boards.

Last month, the volunteer newsletter editor position turned over. I hope the new editor likes my work. Actually, I hope she leaves it alone and doesn't change any of my carefully crafted sentences.

Unless she's my super secret invisible audience.

I profess to writing the book review column for the reading advocacy, for the cerebral activity, and for the online connection to MVMOMs. But I have one more top secret agenda. My greatest motivator is an audience that probably doesn't exist. I could have tossed a jumble of words together every month and the MVMOMs would have awarded Facebook thumbs-up to clunky sentences and awkward phrases. They were all nice, time-crunched ladies who wouldn't have judged me harshly for mixed metaphors or unparallel sentences. So my imagination conjures up a fake target audience.

I agonize over every sentence, every word; just in case one of the MVMOMs reading the newsletter works at a fancy publishing job. This fantasy is not completely out of the realm of reality, I don't think. There are seriously professionally accomplished MVMOMs: lawyers, doctors, academics, and business owners. Why not a big-time book editor or literary agent?

I don't care how dumb this sounds because having an invisible reader to win over makes me a better writer. I always have a side-dream fantasy that I'll be plucked out of a slush pile by someone who sees promise in my writing. A Freudian might attribute this behavior as delusionally compensating for a lack of attention in some aspect of my childhood. And I can trace it to my childhood, but not to where a Freudian might go. I am certain that my desire to please an imaginary reader comes from a combination of watching the film Pretty Woman and reading fashion magazines in my early adolescence.

Pretty Woman premiered in 1990. For girls like me, born in the late 1970s or early 1980s, the Richard Gere and Julia Roberts vehicle was a sleepover VCR stalwart that sent a problematic, Cinderella message that young women need powerful men to recognize their beauty and charm, and ultimately save them from prostitution, poverty, and unflattering skimpy knit dresses.

As a teenager I also read an unhealthy number of fashion magazines that were filled with stories of models being discovered in malls, on trains, and other dull settings where fashion model scout vipers laid in wait for nymphette victims. This was a common trope with endless variations. Later in my adolescence, watching network talk show television, I was deeply affected by the The Late Show bit where David Letterman plucked Stephanie, a young producer, from backstage obscurity, and used her for laughs. Years later he admitted that they had been having an affair with a very unequal power dynamic. Maybe there is something Freudian, actually, to uncover here, but as an adolescent, I didn't understand or care about the sexual aspects of those unequal relationships. I translated the fairy tale fantasy to my own life, thinking that somewhere, someday, someone with power and influence might see beauty and potential in my writing. Currently, as a reluctant stay-at-home mom, the fairy tale functions as inspiration. I pretend that a glamorous publishing magnate MVMOM will read the newsletter, delight in my pithy sentences about board books, and offer me a book deal.

My MVMOM book review column wasn't the first time that writing for an unreal audience motivated me to produce my best work. During my master's degree program, I revised draft after draft of writing assignments for the most aloof professor in the department, a history dude-bro who deigned to teach in the library science program. I attended the program in the mid-2000s, the era of Michael Patrick King and Sex and the City Post-it breakup notes, The Rules, and He's Just Not That Into You. The history dude-bro was the bad boyfriend version of a university professor. He dressed sloppily and didn't shave. He arrived to class late and unprepared. He let students run the discussion instead of presenting an outlined lecture. He didn't learn our names or answer our emails. His impossible-to-impress, messy-hair-don't-care veneer motivated me to work extra hard to try and obtain his unattainable attention and approval. To be clear, this wasn't an academic crush situation. The history dude-bro functioned as a stand-in for all of the literary journals that rejected my post-college short stories, for the MFA admission to which I never applied, the book agents to which I never sent proposals, the publishing houses who would never know I existed. I wanted someone, anyone to see me as smart and prescient, as a talented wordsmith who got lost in library school on the way to the English Department. I wanted, above all else, for someone to praise me for being grammatically correct.

What the history dude-bro lacked in classroom management or professional attire, he made up for in a killer library history syllabus and interesting writing assignments. The fact that research papers were my favorite assignments was another sign that I should have gone to school for writing, but I was trying to be practical and settle on library school as writing-adjacent enough. When I completed papers, I'd pretend they mattered, like I was writing them for The New Yorker or Harper's, any high-prestige, pretentious magazine with a Manhattan address. The history dude-bro held onto our papers until almost the end of the semester, witholding feedback for weeks and weeks, which seemed like a tactic to make me work harder to please or impress him. When he finally handed our work back, he included no comments or grades. At the top of each paper he slapdashed check marks that looked more like lopsided, capital Us; or messy, rudimentary birds in flight drawn by a preschooler. When my best library school friend, Annie, saw his thoughtless acknowledgements of assignment completion, she laughed, "He didn't even read these!"

After preschool pick-up and lunch, I read aloud the entire bear book pile to all three of my kids. Together, we sort the best from the dreck. I identify three suitable books for my "When you're tired of reading Brown Bear, Brown Bear, What Do You See?" theme. I hope it helps MVMOMs burned out on Eric Carle. And showcase my impeccable taste to the MVMOMs who, in my imagination, work as literary agents and high powered publishing executives.

Over two days, I agonize over revisions. Finally, I submit the bear copy and book cover jpeg downloads to my new editor. The old volunteer editor, the one to which I originally pitched my idea, used to send a quick "Thanks!" or no reply at all. So the new editor's lengthy reply surprises me. She writes back with an explanation about how she's decided to change the newsletter's publication schedule from monthly to quarterly. Going forward, she only wants to receive my book review column four times a year. I feel semi-insulted about the downsizing of my monthly column. The new editor's email brings back professional disappointments that still sting, like when I tried to increase my hours at my last reference job at the online school, and my manager could not schedule me for daytime hours because of a hiring freeze. And at my first professional job at the business library, when the board of directors who collectively looked like a group of archetypal cartoon capitalists—Mr. Burns, Mr. Krabs, and the Hasbro Monopoly man—squandered the endowment on pricey consultants and unnecessary technology, then laid off the librarians to balance their budgeting mistakes.

When the new editor's newsletter notification arrives in my email, I open the message and click the link to view the publication, which is hosted on the MVMOM website. I scroll through birth announcements, a club calendar, and the Meet a Member Q+A.

There's my column, which has gone through some kind of editorial version of a barbershop buzz cut wherein the new editor shaved and clipped and plucked away all of my advanced Strunk and White-inspired techniques. The new editor replaced my semicolons with regular-ass commas! Despite the need for semicolons to provide clarity among items in a list! In another book's description, the new editor exchanged an emdash for a colon. What?! She completely misunderstood the point of my emdash—emphasis!—in setting a phrase apart.

Usually my efforts go unnoticed and unappreciated. So I was gobsmacked that the new editor changed my impeccable copy! Removed my Oxford commas! If there was a publishing house bigwig or literary agent phenom lurking in the digital recesses of MVMOM, they'd never scout me out of obscurity, not when the new editor made me look like a boring book reviewer incapable of punctuational flourishes.

I cannot bear the thought of spending so many future hours on crafting tiny paragraphs. Only to have the new editor wield her proverbial red pen—no! A veritable black Sharpie marker over my words and my precious punctuation. My parenthesis and my hyphens! The new editor might as well have highlighted my entire column with her cursor, then selected the Adobe Tools > Redact feature.

My dreams dashed, I cope in the only way I know how. I send a mild-mannered resignation email to the new editor. In a huff, I write:

Great newsletter. I'm so sorry, but I've overcommitted myself with a new volunteer opportunity at my son's preschool. Unfortunately, I can no longer write the book review column for MVMOM.

I leave out my indignation at the new editor's lack of respect for my punctuational integrity. But I sign off with a poorly placed interrobang:

Best of luck and take care?!

Deborah

THESE BONES AT EIGHTY-FOUR

These bones grow brittle
as we age, the limber shock-
absorbing joints of our youth

now gnarled knuckles that
scarcely grip a pencil. And
what of fish bones, skeletons

thin as a wish gone to rest
in mile-deep beds, eons of
deposits morphing into silt.

And birds, holdovers from
the age of dinosaurs, bones so fine
the wind tosses them like confetti

toward the rising sun. Calcium,
copper, iron, boron, phosphorous,
magnesium, zinc, potassium—

stardust seeded in this body we wear
that day by day wends
its way toward the heavens.

SAVINGS

Into our basket small spears of okra,
scarcely beyond bloom; peppers, lobed
at the base, a teasing taste for tomorrow's
pot of chili. We hoard these offerings,
coin against the coming winter.

Once these slight gifts mattered, when we
were young and just beginning, when a forkful
of hay to the cows was a portion earned by our day
in the field, currency of sweat and muscle's effort.

Now freezer holds beans, peas, broccoli, shelves
the jewels of peaches and beets. Still we gather,
spread fruit to ripen on table tops, while cold
creeps along house foundation, finds floor boards
where we stand, juice of the last tomato on our chins.

THE FALSE ALEPH

With apologies to the memory of Jorge Luis Borges

AFTER everyone else leaves the Chacarita cemetery and the gravediggers finish tamping the soil with their spades, the four of us remain behind.

"Carlos Argentino Daneri was a modernist in the worst sense of the word." I crush a cigarette underfoot.

"He exemplified the time," says Adolfo Bioy Casares.

"Many find his poetry obtuse—unable to breath the rarified air—"

"Borges, you're still upset he won second place in the National Prize for Literature. That was in nineteen forty-three—nine years ago, and you try to erase your jealousy by giving him the accolades he never received."

"Think of it as an opportunity to add vigor and vinegar to the Argentine literary canon. Eradication is impossible—placing Daneri in the center of the labyrinth will baffle the man of the future."

"He would be gratified by the comparison to Theseus."

"Or the horned beast haunting the maze that is contemporary society."

"He ignored editorial deadlines and abhorred silence." Silvina Ocampo removes her eyeglasses and dabs at imaginary tears. "An incessant talker. On several occasions I ordered him to shut up. He was oblivious."

I lean against the plain marker and kick at the pile of dirt already dotted with black ants. Next to it is a granite plinth topped with a marble angel, from a time when the Daneri-Viterbo family could afford such monuments to their dead. Bioy and Silvina begin discussing the next issue of Sur.

"Women were attracted to him because of his sadness." Silvina's sister Victoria links arms with me and guides me to a shaded bench. "It was tragic, and therefore, romantic."

"He told me he was born in Ciudad Eva Perón when it was still called La Plata. I think he was trying to impress me."

"His mother abandoned the family when he was young. With the first stirrings of the libido he fell in love with Evita when she was just another pretty actress. I often wonder what that moment was like."

"For women, everything comes back to love."

"And Carlos Argentino?

"He told me of a vision," I say. "A moment when the entire world and everything in it was revealed to him, simultaneously. That glimpse of the infinite pushed him over the edge. His so-called opus was an attempt to reproduce a feverish dream. He called that moment the Aleph and showed it to me once. I merely experienced the shock of the new."

"Jorge Luis." Victoria removes a compact from her purse and gazes at her reflection. She turns the mirror toward me. "Do you hate reflections and reproduction as much as you hate Carlos Argentino?"

"Pine trees shake like wet linen, panther clouds stalk the rain, the light does a turnabout, puddles reflect solar egg yolks—"

"—spring comes with bedsprings and bleached sheets. Ha! I also memorized Equinox. It's one of my favorite poems. Admit it, my friend—the memory of Beatriz is breaking your heart."

She spreads a cloth between us and unpacks a picnic hamper. Empanadas, choripán, milanesas, and alfajores with dulce de leche, oranges, grapes, and plums, sugar cookies, a thermos of coffee, bottles of Cerveza Quilmes.

Our friends sit on a bench next to us.

"A toast," says Bioy. "To the memory of Carlos Argentino Daneri. May his verses outlast his name, and may his name outlast all of us."

We lean together and clink bottles. Victoria, bless her, pours her beer on his grave.

The next morning I scrub soiled pen nibs and align blank sheets of paper. All around me books with damaged spines, torn magazines, and fly-specked windows. Beneath a cracked ceiling tile in the contemporary fiction section a puddle grows fuzzy with mold. A barking cough—I rush through skewed stacks and snatch an explicit anatomy book from a nonagenarian. His drool stains a grainy black and white photo of a female breast. I chase him from the library and return to my desk and the galley proofs for my own soon-to-be-published collection of essays, *Otras inquisiciones*. The critique on Daneri's incomplete opus, *Mi visión del mundo* is incomplete. The final lines of his "Equinox" are the prologue to my essay,

>feral varmints toe-tap the distance from bed to kitchen
>
>this quiet story extracts the pink ululation
>
>twists sheaves of algae into already braided hair

yet my closing quote from one of his early 'nature' poems, "Las pampas", with its ill-timed caesura,

>expect nothing but anticipate, what Argentina reveals
>
>in the blank spaces between what we already know

fails to aesthetically balance the prologue. I resolve to complete the essay before the end of the day. My muse never fails me.

"Beatriz Elena Viterbo." In the library my voice is the whisper of a falling leaf. Her cameo silhouette in my desk drawer, more precious than any globular liquid Aleph. The thrill of possessing a stolen bit of carved ivory which once held place of honor over her heart (O jealousy!) now more important than the raspy cigarette smoker consonants of her voice, more meaningful than the soapy odor of her blouse, more immediate than her eyes—one green, one brown—which looked into one's soul and dismissed what they found there. Her fingers floating over the keys of a virginal like tiny birds—

And then it makes sense, a throwaway passage from Daneri's "Los cielo":

>diffused warbler smoke, careening canyon doves
>
>empty sparrows push new roads and melt intent ravens
>
>they peep inside me like I owe them something

The perfect close to a perfect essay. Bioy, Silvina, and Victoria will be impressed. I cap the inkwell and place it in the drawer, next to the cameo. Black ink, white ivory—the meaning I once gave that contrast escapes me now.

Completion calls for celebration. I telephone Bioy Casares.

"I'm still digesting yesterday's picnic," he says.

"Just you and me." I hide my manuscript in the desk. "Surely you and Silvina can be parted for one or two hours."

My assistant accepts the keys to the rare book cases and I leave for an early lunch.

I disembark from the bus on the far side of the street. Zunino and Zungri's café spreads along one entire block of Calle Garay. Starched businessmen, middle-class married couples, students, and tourists queue outside on the pavement. The home Daneri shared with his cousin Beatriz gone years ago, and with it, perhaps, the Aleph.

On record I've expressed the opinion that Daneri's Aleph was a false Aleph. Yet it was the only one I've ever seen, and if it once truly existed it would still be present on the premises of the café, in the exact spot it occupied when the Daneri-Viterbo house still existed. Perhaps the builders turned the cellar of the house into a storeroom, perhaps they retained the original oak stair steps descending into that underworld of delights. If so, then the false Aleph still exists. This is not philosophy, but logic.

I push through the crowd with excuses. Zunino—one can tell him from his twin by a white scar above his left eyebrow—listens to that logic and simultaneously greets customers, shouts at waiters, and rushes to rearrange chairs and tables.

"I've read your fantastic stories in *Sur*. They are incomprehensible to a working man such as myself. Your request is unusual." He brushes powdered sugar from his silk Italian suit and gestures to the scores of customers and the bustle of digestion. "Come back at two o'clock in the morning, after we close. You can snoop in the cellar all you want. Table for two? Right here by the window so you can study the people and discover what motivates them. That's what you writers do, isn't it?"

Bioy Casares is punctual, smartly appointed, constructively critical.

"Growing a beard, my friend?"

"Is it so important?" I rub my chin and wave a hand at the flotsam at other tables. "Who cares?"

"One woman, and that should be enough."

"Victoria is a dream from the future."

"And Beatriz?"

"Her spirit waits for me to do the correct thing."

"You've been drinking?"

The implication pulls up a third chair. I conveniently ignore it. We discuss my manuscript, and our fourth ongoing collaboration, *Cuentos breves y extraordinarios*.

He drives me back to the library in his Ford sedan, a recent and pretentious acquisition.

At work I am so distracted that when a professor from the university asks for the annotated copy of *St. Augustine's Confessions*, I hand him a copy of De Quincey's *Confessions of an English Opium-Eater*.

As a child the schoolroom clock moved at the speed of melting ice. Today the hands of a clock appear to freeze or slip backwards, tempting me to alter my versions of the past. I tell my coworkers I am staying late. One of them hesitates before turning off the lights and locking the door. I heat coffee on an electric hot plate and nibble dry biscuits. The desk lamp creates a puddle of light and I lose myself in making slight revisions to the *Otras inquisiciones* manuscript.

At one o'clock I step outside. A mild spring rain releases nostalgia trapped in the dust of the streets. The bus is empty and the driver changes his sign to Out of Service. I fortify myself with a sip of laudanum.

The San Cristóbal barrio is half asleep. A dog slinks past under orange street lights and two inebriated men argue outside the café. The waiters and cleaners ignore my knocks. Zungri unlocks the door.

"You are expected and welcome—as long as you don't report us to the health inspector! A joke, Borges, just a joke. Please, sit with me for a few minutes."

He places sugar cubes on slotted spoons over glasses of verte absinthe and dissolves the sugar with drops of water.

"To your health."

"My second toast in forty-eight hours," I say. "Yesterday morning we acknowledged the memory of your nemesis."

"Daneri? I didn't know he died. To Daneri, may he find his sacred elf."

"Aleph. His sacred Aleph. If it still exists in your cellar."

"Honestly? I think you're insane. I'm practical yet compassionate to a fault."

"I may be down there quite a while."

"The night watchman can let you out," says Zungri. "Zipacna makes sure nobody runs off with the silverware. I'm joking, Borges!"

My memory of the cellar is at odds with the reality. I see myself—a middle-aged librarian in a brown linen blazer stretched out on the floor, watched over by a curious and angelic kitchen staff above me.

"Turn out the lights, please, and close the door," I say. "Complete darkness is necessary."

I'm not surprised, and yet—I am surprised.

The Aleph is as I remember it, precise and untarnished.

Faces, colors, names, fish, tents, caravans, black crepe, cinnamon bark, Ulrikke leading me to a loft, a bar of sulfur in a steamer trunk, languid afternoon curtains above mismatched lovers, the inky letters of a business card, horses on the pampas, an abattoir steaming with blood, alien deserts and full moons, crowded streets and incandescent lights, a knife fight, an Arctic midnight sun, marketplace watermelons, Aztec temples scored with hairline cracks, sprigs of anise, a bowl of American baked beans, ice on the Seine, pulsing arteries on the back of a woman's hands, a billboard on the Plaza Constitución, sunflowers, the muddy banks of Río de la Plata, a lecture hall in Paris, dirigibles above Bonn, a glistening snail in a moonlit garden, myself clutching a framed photograph of Beatriz.

Was it the men who demolished Daneri's house? The builders with their drills and hammers? Or merely the minutely shifting earth and the passage of time? The false Aleph is cracked, fractured, and distorted. It is the difference between a midnight chorus and a well-tuned symphony.

A ghostly hand brushes my cheek. When I reach to touch it, it undergoes a metamorphosis and becomes a beetle. The illuminated pantheon dissolves, fractures into chipped granite angels and stained marble cherubs.

Death's archetype opens the door and descends the steps. His black hooded cloak, glinting scythe, and shifting hourglass.

"Señor Borges!" Zipacna grinds dust beneath his feet. "I was told to keep an eye on you. Are you ready to come up for air? This? I'm off to a fancy dress party and only waiting on you. Excuse my saying so, but a man of your position and age shouldn't be lying about in damp cellars."

"I'm finished."

"Want to come along? My girlfriend has a sister—"

We part outside the café. I've forgotten about the buses—five kilometers to the library and twenty-plus to my flat. I don't have a choice. My footsteps echo from hard walls.

The night is revelers, honking horns, and the occasional sound of breaking glass. Exhausted, I make a promise to myself to begin the calisthenic exercises that Victoria recommended. I consider the wisdom of wandering the streets of Buenos Aires by night or by day.

My desk drawer quivers with anticipation. The manuscript of *Otras inquisiciones* flickers with St. Elmo's fire. Flames fill my sleeves and trousers, ignite a truthfulness that the heart refuses to accept.

I think I will never sleep again, even as it overtakes me.

A drool stain on my blotter. Strong sunlight burns away gold leaf book titles. Hexagonal library rooms recede to vanishing points in all directions and fold in on themselves, a loop the scientists claim is infinity, defined. The cleaner nudges my shoulder.

"Señor Borges." She plunges a mop into a bucket. "That's the fifth time this month. Working late and sleeping at your desk. It's none of my business, but isn't it time you married and settled down?"

My rumpled suit and unshaven cheeks—people on the morning bus glance and turn away. I must look awful. The cemetery markers are spotted with moss, industrial dust, and bird feces.

Carlos Argentino Daneri's grave is overshadowed by Beatriz Elena Viterbo's angelic monument. I turn the cameo in my hand—it clicks and folds open to reveal a compartment I never knew existed.

Inside is a mirror all of two centimeters in diameter. Reflected there is the source and conclusion of my solitary journey.

INSTANT

A white-tailed deer strides into
the Wissahickon, stops mid-stream,
bordered by water, framed by trees.

My eye clicks like a latch as I create
a holding of this time and place,
my own box containing a deer shape

joined with a lack of breeze, sweat
salting my lips, dots of humming
insects and shade like blue weather.

Before sleep, between tasks, whenever
my hold on the immediate slackens,
I return to that image. I see her bend

to the water, sip, and raise up,
each movement a natural fragment,
a chapter in a story from another life.

ODE TO MY BREASTS

I have no memory of the buds, the hard fists
of hormones hauling you up not unlike
the earth moved by velvety voles.
Warm friends, I underestimated you.
You grew out of sinewy muscle and fat,
that dirty word, that dense tissue
why they call you now to annual auditions
for which I hope you never get the role.
How often I hid you under sweatshirts, bound
you inside my leotard. When the first man
let his mouth linger on your soft edges,
I listened to your song for the first time.
And when you hardened like stones after childbirth,
I cursed you until I saw how my babies
relied on your rich milk, creamy and unrelenting.
For years you overflowed, spilled
into their hungry mouths without ever taking a bow.
Now that they drink from a carton and forage
for love in the thick forest of adolescence,
you are not to be pitied. You may feel obsolete,
but I still adore your sensual shape –
the way you yearn to be touched, suffer
the smallest let down when an infant draws near.

WASHED-OUT HORNS

WHEN Sig started quoting Bob Dylan, like the words to the songs actually fit what was happening, I tried to get away. I liked it better when he was drinking, when he was showing off and not just trying to show off. With Sig there was a difference. It wasn't right, seeing him act like he knew something he didn't, understood something he hadn't even listened to. Then again, I had seen him do worse. I tried not to think about that. I didn't want it to ruin another good night.

There was a midnight festival up by the river and I went there early, before dinnertime, to take in the sun and the wind before too many people showed up, and Sig was already there. He didn't see me. He was talking to a couple of German girls who were in town for the summer. I had spent the night before talking to one of them over at the Copper Corner but I drank too much and when I went outside for some fresh air I forgot to go back and follow up on my luck. Now Sig was at them, telling him that he did twenty years of schooling and couldn't even get the day shift. Jesus Christ.

I looked at Sig and the girls laughing, and wondered if he would pied-piper them away, too, like he had with Erin. Why did he have to be the one that came back to town? Sometimes I thought he was singlehandedly draining the town of all it's women. He didn't even mean to, they just looked at him and either went away with him on one of his broken jaunts down south or they looked at him, looked at those happy blue eyes, and started thinking about how much better their life could be, if only. I don't even know what 'if only' but there was something in his eyes that got women dreaming.

It was a bright day and a strong wind cut out through the mountains and still held a touch of frost. Even over all the festival noise I could hear the river run. The ravens were out, watching everyone. They looked like they were waiting on something but I couldn't figure out what. And the air smelled of those Czech sausages that Emil's father was grilling. I spent most of the festival avoiding Sig. I got close enough a few times to hear him talk, hear him quote Dylan or go into one of his stories about the rodeos down south. I was glad no one was serving any beer. He would have started telling everyone about his dreams then, hoping it would get more beer flowing his way. And it always worked, too. It drove me nuts. Why the hell did people want to hear about his dreams so badly? They hadn't meant anything for years, not since I was a kid.

Just before midnight I ran into Stella. She was hiding a bag of red wine in her purse and we drank it, sitting in the grass, not really talking, and I fell asleep listening to girls laugh.

WHEN I was a kid, my father still spent the winters in town. Or close to it. Sometimes he stayed with us for a little, at least until the air bristled with tension between him and my mother, and sometimes he got a room or small apartment. Once or twice, he spent a few months motel hopping out on the highways. I found out years later than he usually skipped out on the bills and then settled them up come summer, when he got riding or digging again and had enough money to go around. Half the time people just let him off the hook, though. I don't know how he managed that. No one could afford that kind of loss. He didn't even need to sing them a hard luck song.

Word got around that he was something else on a horse, winning events down south and everything, and he got to stay out at the Horse Shoo, in the caretakers' cabin. The manager looked like some old gunfighter and even smelled of what my father called black powder smoke, but during the winter he came and went and kept his distance from the stables and from my father and anything that looked like work. My father called him Mr Clark but said that wasn't his real name. I tried to avoid him because he always looked at me like something was wrong. I took it personal.

I liked the caretakers' cabin. It was old and there were even holes in the wall – at twelve I was sure they were old bullet holes – so that frozen winter wind just ripped right through, but my father plugged them up with wet newspaper that froze over and the whole placed smelled of stale wool and horses. The stables were about fifty feet away and when I spent the night and the weather got bad, I could hear the horses kicking up a storm in the stalls. The electric came and went so my father used kerosene lanterns even during the day. At that time of year there wasn't much difference between night and day anyway and I would spend hours in his bed reading a book called *The Old Curiosity Shop* that Gwyn had left behind. I had trouble getting past the first two pages, but they were a good first two pages.

I still missed Gwyn. Or at least I thought about her a lot. After she had gone, I kept going out to the shack she had been staying in, but I didn't spend the night there anymore, not without her. I went through the place, went through the few things that were left behind and took what had been hers. There wasn't much. A bottle of scotch with one inch left over that I took home and stashed under my bed; a few wooden bears and an old shirt that smelled but I kept it close anyway. And the book. One night when I was out there, I thought about how my father was always finding old pistols way back when. Once it got him arrested, but after that, after I had come along, he just seemed to turn up with them, like it was normal for him to be looking around an old farmhouse's crawl space or behind walls and under floorboards. He never hung on to them, he didn't know what to do with them, and they just slipped away; traded in for half a package of cigarettes or an inch of scotch. He would have looked at Gwyn's loot and thought that some people had all the luck. She would have thought the same thing about him. I was just glad that a girl like Gwyn wasn't going around finding old weapons. Jesus Christ.

Finally, the winter came on hard and they closed off the roads so the snow got too high to walk through. But by then I was spending a lot of time out at the Horse Shoo with my father.

WHEN I woke up the festival had petered out. Stella was gone but I was holding the bag of wine and there was still a little in there. I blinked at the daylight, the sun up too early, and looked around. A few people were carrying on, too tired to have any real fun, but dragging it out anyway. The stalls had been folded up and packed away, the stage was empty, but wine and a few cases of beer had been brought out of hiding. I took a sip of Stella's wine. It shook me up.

A skinny woman I met a few years back, when I was down south working a rodeo I had fallen into, was playing her fiddle quietly for a group of blank-faced locals, but I didn't know if it was real because I thought she had been killed not long after I met her. Poisoned for sleeping with the married owner of the saloon she used to play in. At least that's what I heard. But people tell a lot of stories.

Sig was still there. Of course. Sitting with a girl who had been working at the donut store all summer. She had really nice eyes and I had even made her laugh once or twice when I had gone in early for coffee, before too many people showed up and ruined the place. I smiled because I knew he was barking up the wrong tree. The girl was too smart for his lines. She didn't even like Dylan, told me once it was all just moaning and groaning that unhappy kids listened to. I took my coffee and donut from her and grinned, told her she was right, and thought she was too young to be calling anyone else a kid.

Sig was looking at me. He didn't look away either, and I felt like a damn jack rabbit in a fox den. What the hell did he want?

The girl took Sig's hand and kept talking to him. She leaned against him a little and I saw that faraway look on her face.

He stood up, still looking at me, and walked over. His work shirt was open to the last two buttons, showing the scars along his ribs where he had been stepped on when he was showing off after he'd already come second in one of the big rodeos, and he got a cigarette going. He sat down next to me and the air fogged up with nicotine, old beer and the oiled smell of animal skins.

He reached for Stella's wine and I let him take it. I was done drinking anyway.

"Sig," I said.

He shook his head. There was a cold wind and I thought summer would be shorter than usual this year. "Why do you always call me that?" he asked.

"It's your name, isn't it."

"Yeah." He took another sip of the wine. "I'm looking for some help with a job."

"I'm not looking for work."

"You're never looking for work."

"Well, I don't need any."

"You don't need any? I heard you lost your truck."

"I didn't lose it." How do you tell a guy like Sig you gave it away?

Sig started laughing softly and I wondered what he already knew.

I DON'T think Gwyn ever told me the truth about anything. She didn't have it in her. It didn't matter though. I still knew what I saw. Or what I dreamed. That was real. That was true. And she got me talking. It was all nerves on my part, but she pushed it, got me thinking, so that I got ideas in my head that I knew somehow, some day, I would follow through.

Back then, my mother was still making the two of us those Sunday night dinners and on Mondays I took leftovers out to Gwyn and we sat out front of the hunting shack, on logs I had sawn down and rolled close together, and ate cold fried chicken. She could really eat. I don't know how she was so thin. And the way she licked her lips to clean away the chicken always got to me. She caught me looking sometimes and teased me a little by biting her lip or licking it slowly. I pretended I had no idea what she was doing and went back to my chicken and told her about how I was going save up; hitch rides down to Texas to work the bulls next summer, maybe she should stick around and come with me. If she had stayed, I might have done it, too. And not because it was what I wanted to do.

"Next summer? By then I'll be long gone."

It hurt a little to hear her say that. "Where to?"

I liked listening to Gwyn's plans. Even if they weren't real. Maybe I just liked listening to her voice. Once in a while she'd get quiet and hold my hand and look out at the trees, seeing something in her head. If she held on to me too long, she'd suddenly let out a short laugh and tell me

I was alright for a kid, like she was so much older than me.

The cabin at the Horse Shoo reminded me of her. I thought it was the kind of place she'd have liked. But I had a good history of being wrong.

And I spent a lot of time alone out at the Horse Shoo too, like I had at Gwyn's. There wasn't a lot of work to do over the winter but my father would head out early to do one chore or another, and then sometimes I wouldn't see him for a day or two. I didn't tell my mother. I don't know where he went. He didn't seem to know either. He wasn't drinking then. I wondered if he had been out chasing down a dream, but I didn't ask him.

With my father coming and going like that I got worried about the horses. Their water froze up overnight and they couldn't drink. If I wasn't around to break up the ice and throw hay at them, I didn't know if they'd make it, so I started to wake early when I was in town and thumb a ride in the dark up to the Horse Shoo and when my father found out he moved a bedroll into the barn and started sleeping in there, whether or not I was spending the weekend with him, and sometimes I'd walk into the barn in the morning to check on him and the horses both and I'd see him sleeping in an empty stall and I got the feeling he liked it more than the cabin, that it made him feel like he was out rambling again. The cabin was too much home for someone like my father.

I DID need the work. Even if it was with Sig. All the same, I spent three days scurrying around town, avoiding bars and empty doorways, wishing I could hightail it out of town in a truck I didn't have, before I knuckled down and went looking for him. He was easy to find.

Stella was covering for the summer at the Copper Corner and when I walked in, she looked up at me and started laughing. I didn't know why. Sig was sitting across from her, leaning into the bar, talking about how great her hair was. He still smelled of cigarettes and horses. The smell always stayed with him, like they were in him, even when he had gone months without getting near a horse. Stella shook her hair out without noticing. Sig did that to people. He was right, though, she did have great hair. The kind that every redhead wants. Or maybe that was just me.

There wasn't anybody else in the bar and I wondered why they were listening to Waylon Jennings. At least it wasn't Dylan. Things were looking up.

I sat down and Stella put a bottle of Coors in front of me. I looked at the mountains on the label. As soon as I saved up enough for a new truck I'd head off, lose myself for a few weeks in mountains that looked like that. There was a lot I wanted to save up for. Over the years I kept inching toward a plot of land up off the highway to Cubby Hill, where there was a solid trailer-home that looked out over low parkland that no one ever used. Two years ago some kid moved in for the summer and built a stone firepit behind the trailer. Did a good job of it, too. No one ever seemed to stay there more than a few weeks and that was in the summertime only. Half the roads were closed off in the winter and when I drove by I liked the way the trailer sat there, so much white sky behind it, far from anywhere, far from anyone. It looked like a hell of a place to live. But that kind of money was a long way off.

"Change your mind about the job?" Sig asked.

"I don't know. Tell me about it."

"Nothing to it." He tapped his bottle and Stella put down a new one. I wondered how far along he was. With Sig, it could be hard to tell. "Search and rescue."

"Jesus Christ."

"You know Dan Plummer?" he asked.

"I know who he is."

"He needs a hand tearing down the old structures at his place by Moon Ridge."

Moon Ridge got my back up. People said Moon was short for Moonshine, because people used to make booze up there and got even richer than the miners they sold to, until it all went bloody. But then people told a lot of stories. Only a handful were true.

"Plummer needs a hand?" I asked.

"Needs someone to do it. I'm the one that needs a hand." He finished his new beer. Just like that. And asked for another one. It meant he had money this time. "The buildings are nearly a hundred years old. They'll come down easy."

"I thought they came down years back. Hit by a storm or something."

"A couple did. I was there when it happened."

I looked at Sig. I got a bad feeling, but then he told me how much the job paid.

My father's dreams came in bouts. When he was in a dry spell, he just sort of muddled through the world, a little lost, looking for words and what to do next. It was alright though; back then, he knew when to shut up. And so it got quiet in the caretaker's cabin. Sometimes I forgot we were both there. More often than not, we weren't both there. It was just me. Me and my memories of Gwyn. I kept holding on to those, replaying them, trying to see her again, trying to spend more time with her, even if only in my head.

She had made it halfway through the book. There were creases, really small ones, on the tops of the pages where she marked her place. When she was still in the hunting shack, I liked watching her read, but it never lasted long. She'd catch me out, like I was doing something wrong, and throw the book at me, and then she'd show me how to make a tinder stick. She told me I wasn't any good at it, and took my hands and guided the knife along the wood and I tried to make sure she didn't notice my brain exploding every time she touched me. Her hands were rough, especially for a kid. I guessed it was from all the time she spent trying to carve out those wood bears that lined the windowsills of the shack. She really dug into the wood. I was pretty sure there was something else going on.

I dreamed about her, too. And when I did, I was glad my father wasn't around. He would have seen it all over my face.

When I woke up, after dreaming long and hard about Gwyn, I knew she was far away. She wouldn't stop either, not for a long time. Talk about jealous. The sun was still down but there was a blue buzz out the window, over the snow; morning moving slow, and I went to water the horses. There were six of them, all a little shaggy and bored from the long winter. I cracked the ice with a shovel and turned on the water, then I looked in the empty stall where my father kept a bedroll, but it was empty.

He was gone again.

Sometimes, if a dream hit my father right, he started out right away. My mother had told me about a time or two when he would just up and go, drive through the snow all night or pack up and walk into Deerfoot Valley or over near McGill where the mines had been before it all went south. Once he found a skull with eight gold teeth and another time, he found a case of whiskey when he fell into an old cellar. After a dream, he kept going until he found what he was after. He always knew it was out there, knew that he was right. Some days later he'd turn up on Steele Street, outside Anton's, waiting for him to open so that he could sell whatever he had in his pockets.

I spent five or six days looking around the woods near Horse Shoo. At night, alone in the cabin, I read *The Old Curiosity Shop* and ate scrambled eggs and tried not to think about how sometimes my father went out and didn't come back for a year.

A few days later I woke up in the night and my mother was there. She took me home and we didn't mention my father, but I kept running through the dreams he had told me, thinking that I might be able to follow them, find him.

I HAD been stuck in town for a couple of months. It made me itchy. When the wind blew, I wanted to go with it. One night I said something vague about it at the Copper Corner and Stella snorted, told me I was turning into my father. I left without finishing my drink.

The first two weeks in town I stayed with my mother but after a bit the two of us started huffing around the house like a couple of bulls penned in too tight, and Mrs. Luther, next door, kept asking me to fix her plumbing and after I did, she told me what was wrong with my work and that I had to do it again. She paid me in day old casserole, though, so it wasn't the worst deal, but then she started acting like she was doing me a favour.

Griff didn't let me stay at the campground because of the summer tourism and after a few nights in the park Roy Lanksy saw me and told me to watch his place while he was down south playing cards, but it was right in town, half a block from Main Street. I could hear cars and people and that weird hum of town all night long. It freaked me out. Made it hard to breathe. I wondered if the park would be better. And I looked forward to getting out of town, even if it was just Moon Ridge, and even if it was with Sig.

When Sig picked me up in the morning at the donut shop, hands full off coffee and a box of chocolate glazed, he was driving Plummer's truck. It was one of those new Chevy's, all big tires and shiny paint. Give it a week, I thought. Sig could take the shine out of a diamond.

I looked at the donuts. It was an even dozen. "Who else is coming?" I asked.

"Just us." Sig looked back at the shop and waved at the girl behind the counter.

"You know she's not on commission, right? You and me don't need more than one or two."

"I got a sweet tooth," he said.

"Right."

"And Plummer's picking up the tab."

I wondered where else Plummer would be picking up the tab.

It took a while to get out to Moon Ridge. Sig drove like a geriatric. I had never been out there before, so I just sat back and let him hum along, watched the mountains grow.

Moon Ridge was off a valley full of Jack Pine and a creek ran through it, shallow and fast. Most of the land had been cleared a long time ago. A few birch and scrub managed to grow up near the main house, which wasn't much considering the Plummers. I had seen the inside of their home in Whistle Flat. I didn't know if the main house was coming down too, but it would be a big job, especially with just me and Sig. I wondered if he had talked himself into more than he could chew. It wouldn't be the first time. There were three outbuildings still standing, but not by much. They were all thin grey wood and broken windows. I tried to remember if I had ever crashed in one for a few days during some winter. They had that look. Gwyn would have been at home there.

Sig got out of the truck and looked around. He smiled and nodded to himself.

I took a donut and watched him. Part of me was waiting for the other foot to fall.

"Why's Plummer want to take all this down?" I asked. "He rebuilding?"

"Sort of," Sig said. "We got to talking one night at the Inn. He took me on as what you might call an advisor."

"To advise him in what?" I thought he was hired to knock stuff down.

Sig winked at me. I wanted to tell him I wasn't one of his barmaids.

"Remember I told you I shacked up here during a storm some years back?"

"Yeah." Over the years Sig had shacked up pretty well everywhere.

"I found a hidden basement. Got two cases of eighty-year-old whiskey out of it."

Everyone knew that story. "What'd you do with them?"

He didn't answer, and I figured he drank them. Might have even made it all last a week.

"I also found a gold-digging licence from '99," Sig said. "You know nothing was ever found here, right?"

"Nothing to find," I said. I looked around. "Not around here. That's why the moon shine."

Sig shook his head. "You think Plummer knows that?"

Plummer never struck me as dumb. Just rich. And that's not the same thing.

I DIDN'T go out to the Horse Shoo again for a few weeks. My mother made me go to school and mostly I went. I didn't like school, especially in wintertime. The lights were just too bright inside. Winter was meant to be dark. After class, when it was dusk for a few hours, I checked the woods behind the house for animals. If I went far enough, sometimes I found the bones of small fry, the little animals that were easy pickings, and I brought them back to school and gave them to my biology teacher for what she called extra credit, but when I saw my grades I never knew where that credit had actually gone. Either way, she had a good collection of skulls and jaws from beaver and birds and racoons along her windowsill that made the classroom more tolerable. Once, I found a half-eaten ermine near the river, all white with winter and red with blood, but there was too much flesh to bring it to school so I put it in my desk at home until it smelled and my mother threw it away and cuffed me for being an idiot. It took weeks for the smell to go away. But it made my bedroom feel a little like the caretaker's cabin, a little like a place that Gwyn might have liked, so I didn't mind.

My mother told me not to worry about the horses, Mr Clark was still around, in and out of town like he did during winter, and he'd figure out about my father soon enough and know how to handle it. I thought about the gun powder smell of his and about how a man like that handled things.

Every so often I asked my mother if she knew where my father was, if he was back yet, but she just chewed her lip and thought so long about what to say to me that I got bored and left.

Sig's dreams had enough history behind them that I was sure I knew what had happened; he had followed one of them. I just had to figure out which one.

Earlier that winter my father told me a row of dreams about dead horses. It didn't seem to help him remember to do his job, but it set his mind off, wondering what was going on. When I asked my mother what part of town dead horses were kept in, she gave me that look again and shook her head and told me to go outside and play.

"It's nearly thirty below."

"That's never stopped you before."

I started to put on my coat.

"Wait," she said. "If you do go outside, where are you going to go?"

I shrugged.

"You aren't going to go look for dead horses, are you?" She took a look at me. "Jesus Christ. The weasel was bad enough. Go upstairs and read your book."

And I did. A little. Mostly the part about the old man walking alone at night. He was right. Night time is the best time for walking. I wasn't allowed out at real night, but it was dark so early it was almost the same thing just walking home from school.

My father had also told me a dream about meeting the Queen of England in the Silverload mine. He liked that one. No one had ever found anything in Silverload. This really got him going. He wondered why people dumped so much time and money into looking there in the first place. There must have been something about it, he said. I heard about that kind of thing happening every few years. Old claims deemed nothing but dirt because no one looked hard enough, dug deep enough, stayed sober enough. Or to hear my father tell it, they shot each other before anyone found anything.

I asked around at school. No one seemed to know where dead horses were kept, but I knew where Silverload was, and I started thinking about how to get out there. It was too far to walk in winter but I gave it a shot anyway. It was only thirty below.

SIG surprised me. He picked me up early every morning at the donut shop and when we got out to Moon Ridge, he worked hard. And he knew what he was doing. Not that taking down a house needed much know-how, but he stopped me from bringing a wall and a staircase down on my own head. He opened his first can of beer early, when the wind was still cold with night, but he paced himself.

I liked being out there, at Moon Ridge. Away from town. Sig paid me at the end of every day at first and I tucked the money away. After the first week was over, he said he'd pay me every three or so days. He looked away when he said it, but I figured if he drank my pay, I could just go straight to Plummer.

The out buildings were old. Brittle and bare from a hundred years of bad weather. One more good windstorm would knock them down. Mostly it was tearing the boards out of the frame, and cutting it down so we could burn it later. It would be a hell of a fire. I hoped I would be around for that.

The main house was going to be more of a problem. The front door was locked but I kicked it open to look around. I didn't know why Plummer wanted that one torn down. It was in good shape. Work had been done on it over the years, too. It seemed like a waste. Even the staircase that led to the small bedroom upstairs was pretty new. I looked out the window, at all the land, at Sig going at one of the old barn walls with a sledge hammer, dust and wood splintering out all around him, and I wondered what Plummer had planned. I couldn't see him putting in a mine, tearing up the land with those hydraulic hunters. I thought about the fire again.

I also got to thinking that instead of staying at Roy's, where I never really slept, I could just stay out at Moon Ridge. When I ran it by Sig, he gave me the thumbs up. The next day I brought out my pack and sleeping bag and set up on the front porch of the main house, out of the wind. I never thought to ask where Sig was staying. Mostly I didn't want to know because then I'd probably have to do something about it, but at the end of the day when he drove off in Plummer's truck and I was alone at Moon Ridge, I got a small campfire going, used up some of the old barn door, and fried a half dozen eggs for dinner and was glad to be able to breathe right again.

Come morning it was raining heavy and Sig didn't show. I took it easy, glad for a day off, and glad to be so far out, at Moon Ridge. I thought Plummer was nuts. Who'd tear up a place like that? Pine snapped in the wind and the rain kept coming but I was safe under the porch, in my sleeping bag.

Sig didn't show for a few days. I lost track of how many. The weather was good again, if a little cold for summer, but I liked it. And there was a lot of wind and it just kept blowing. I got a lot of work done, but didn't start on the main house.

When I ran out of food, I walked into town. It took the better part of the day and it was a little after nine when I got to the Copper Corner. Even from outside the bar I could hear Dylan singing *Sad Eyed Lady of the Lowlands*. Sig played that when he wanted to make a move on someone. I pushed through the door. Sig was in there, leaning close to Stella, making her laugh. I wished she were laughing at him, but knew that wouldn't be true.

She brought me a Coors and I drank it down.

"You're thirsty," Sig said.

I nodded. Watched Stella walk away and turn to look back at Sig. Jesus Christ.

"That's one pretty woman," he said.

I looked at her and my mind wandered. "She's no Peggy Flemming."

Sig looked at me and after a minute he grinned, "You're not thinking about Peggy Fleming?"

How the hell did he know?

I held my bottle up and Stella brought me a fresh one. This time she stayed with us.

"You two strike it rich, yet?" She asked.

"On this job?" I laughed.

"Why not?" she said. "If Plummer thinks it's a sure thing." She trailed off.

"What does Plummer think is a sure thing?" I asked.

She pointed at Sig. "His track record."

Track record of what? Sig was doing alright this time, this week, but it wouldn't last. Everyone knew it, even if they didn't admit it. Soon he'd be sleeping in doorways and stealing half empty beer bottles at baseball games.

Stella leaned into us. Well, into Sig. I was glad there was a bar between them. "Remember when he kept dreaming about the Woodford Hills? He was in here every night, trying to get backing for it. Here or over at the Buffalo Bar."

"How do you know about that?" I asked. "We were fifteen?"

"And I was here every night, then, too."

"It was like twenty years ago. It's just another old story now."

"But still," She got that look in her eye, gave Sig the hard once over. He was used to it; let her take her time, let her remember him back then.

"He might have dreamed about Woodford, but he sure didn't make anything out of it." He had been arrested for stealing horse manure and spent a few weeks in a cell and when he got released, he went south to rodeo. Come October a professional went digging in Woodford and by the following summer it was one of the big operations with machinery banging away and heavy money filling other people's pockets. "Anyway, what the hell does that have to do with Moon Ridge?"

Stella looked at me like I was an idiot. "He's having those dreams again."

I turned to Sig. He hadn't had a real dream in years. We both knew it. "God damn it, Sig."

I WAS thinking about my father too much, thinking about Gwyn too much, and I lost track of everything. I turned up to school on a Saturday morning and the janitor yelled at me. Also, all my father's dreams had worked their way into me, so that even when I was awake, I dreamt about dead horses, too. Mine were in town, lying dead on the sidewalk. When I walked away from school, I was worried I'd find the streets littered with horses, so I walked out of town instead, turned up toward the highway. It was cold and there was a lot of snowfall on the roads and I decided it was as good a time as any to head up the road and see if I could make it to Silverload. Maybe my father would be there. It would only take a couple of days to walk if the highway had been cleared.

It wasn't cleared. The snow went right up to my knee with every step. It would take a long while to get all the way to Silverload but I didn't have anything else to do.

I hunched down into the wind and kept walking. It felt good, even with the wind full of ice. I liked the burn on my cheeks. And I thought about finding my father out at the old mine, thought about helping him and the two of us coming home with our pockets full. I had been with him once or twice before when he made a good find, a really solid weight. It was a good feeling. It was like finding a few extra months of life for the dead.

Soon the daylight went. I thought about Gwyn, wondered how far south she had gone. If she was even going south, like she told me. She told me a lot of things. Too many of them didn't ring true. I didn't like that. And I didn't like how I still thought about her. I guess there was something else, something inside her, that just kicked me around the right way.

There was a lot of uphill out on the highway. And it was quiet. I liked it. The whole world had gone away.

It was late when headlights came toward me. The truck was coming slow, taking its time in all the snow. I thought about how Gwyn told me she used to slip away into the trees when a car came.

I just stood there.

It pulled up a few feet from me and waited. When the window came down, I walked up to it. Mr Clark looked at me. He had a sharp face, all dark eyebrows and dark thoughts. He still smelled like a shotgun.

"What the hell are you doing way out here?" he asked.

"Going to Silverload."

"In the middle of the night? On foot?"

"I don't drive."

He reached out and opened the door for me. "Get in."

"Silverload is the other direction."

"I know that. I'm not taking you to Silverload. I'm taking you home."

"But my father is out at Silverload."

"What?" He frowned at me.

"He was dreaming about it."

Mr. Clark nodded. "Okay. Well, I'm still taking you home. Otherwise, it'd be third degree murder to leave you out here."

I thought he meant he would kill me. He looked pretty serious about it so I got in and we drove back to town. I had walked for ten, maybe twelve hours, but it took ten minutes to drive. That didn't seem right.

"What are you moping about?" he asked.

"I was already nearly there."

"What? At Silverload. No, you would have been walking all week."

I shrugged. He looked me over. I wondered what he had been shooting to smell like he did.

When we drove through town he had to go slow. The snowploughs were finally out, clearing the roads. We got stuck behind one on Steele Street and when we passed the Buffalo Bar I saw my father, sitting in the doorway, his head against the wall that people always peed on. Someone opened the door and shoved him aside with their foot.

PLUMMER must have known that Sig was a liar. Who didn't? Even so, somehow, when it came to those dreams of his, people still got caught up, even someone smart like Plummer. So, I let it go.

With Stella staying close to Sig all night, bringing him beer after beer so they both lost count, I knew I'd be on my own for a while. Even in the darkness of the bar I could see that Stella was getting that heavy look in her eyes, like she didn't want to keep them open anymore. Sig slid me the keys to Plummer's truck and wandered over to the jukebox. When *Lay Lady Lay* came on, I got the hell out of there.

I stopped by Paddington's for groceries and then dropped them off at my mother's but she was out. She always took extra shifts when Sig was in town. I thought it was because she was nervous about him coming by the house, but one time I dropped a hitchhiker off at the Inn and I saw Sig and my mother sitting at a table by the riverfront window, drinking coffee, grinning at each other. It was a small town. He knew where to find her. And she looked like she liked it.

The weather stayed good for a few days so I worked out at Moon Ridge by myself. It was better that way. I got more done. I didn't have to worry about where Sig was in his drinking, worry about him buzzing another finger off with the electric saw. And I cooked a steak over the campfire every night. I couldn't remember the last time I'd had enough money to eat steak three nights in a row.

At night I got the fire going really big. I liked the way it whipped in the wind, the way the sparks popped in the dark. And there was a lot of wood that needed burning. I got a bit carried away. Watching a fire can do that.

When the fire fell in on itself, with the wind blowing hard enough to smoke my eyes, I didn't notice it had reached the porch of the main house. By the time I looked over, my sleeping bag was up in smoke and most of the porch, too.

I grinned. How slow can a man be? Why was I taking the buildings down plank by plank and burning them, when I could just burn it all outright. Save my back. Get the whole job done in a couple of hours.

I moved the truck back up the driveway and sat on the hood to watch the house burn. Watching a whole house go to flame is something. My bonfire looked like a Zippo next to it.

An hour later, when two trucks from the fire department showed up, most of the house was gone, but the fire was still licking the wind.

I told them not to worry about the house. They hosed the earth around it to stop the fire spreading and then stood there with me for a while, watching the whole thing. I think they liked it, too.

One of them got a cigarette going. "You squatting out here?" he asked.

"What? No. Dan Plummer hired me. He think's Moon Ridge is the next Woodford Hills." Everyone knew about Woodford Hills, even if they didn't know about Sig. Then again, most people knew about Sig, too.

"Moon Ridge?"

"Yeah," I said. "They used to make moonshine out here. The name stuck."

"This isn't Moon Ridge. That's about forty minutes west of here."

"This isn't Moon Ridge?"

He gave me a long look and told his partner to go call the police.

AT LAST, WHAT EVE UNDERSTOOD

After a 15th century manuscript illumination

Adam is oblivious, crouching down to name
yet another unnamed blade of grass,

while the Serpent Girl, walking still,
approaches Eve and will seem to her

almost like a child-like version of herself:
the same small breasts, lank blonde hair,

the same eager gaze. And perhaps what makes it
all inevitable is the warm breath Eve feels

against her cheek, the words the creature speaks
so clearly: *You will now be wise.*

And so, Eve puts aside her fear. She eats and learns—
eats and understands—

thorns and thistles it shall bring forth for you—

by the sweat of your brow—

you are dust and to dust you shall return—

as if all of it were hers to see. But even beyond
the garden's gate, beauty is never entirely gone.

These things endure: long evening light,
green on the surface of a sea—

a small dark bird flying low over the yellow field—
sun that enters morning's open door and her husband's

lovely hand, rough and lined with age.
Of course, she knows failure now. And friendless hours.

But doesn't time, where she must live, have its gifts?
Memory returns the face of the brother she has lost.

She is like a woman who spends an afternoon with a box
of old photographs, choosing images from years before —

in this one, she is dark-haired, smiling,
posed with her daughter in some sandy spot long past.

And she will say, *Yes, I still remember that day.*
How warm the sun is on her skin! And how

her own child is forever cradled in her arms,
among those remnants of the garden ever green.

SCALING MOUNT WHITMAN: LEAVES OF GRASS AND AMERICA'S FIRST GREAT 'AWOKENING'

CARDS on the table. I'm not a Whitman scholar. Put me down, I guess, as a plain old reader who likes literature. As I've gotten older, I've found myself constructing in my head a short list of books that loom in the readerly distance, their commanding heights something of a beckoning taunt. Some need to scale Mount Everest or float down the Mississippi. My "Kilimanjaro before I die" obsessions have more often than I'd care to admit focused on books. Perhaps a function of my small-town upbringing in the South long decades ago, reading provided an escape from a culturally and racially stultified setting and a spur to shove off for eventually fairer, freer shores. Reading also allowed me in those days to enact my little dramas of cultural self-improvement and dream of one day writing like Nabokov or Baldwin. In tribute to – or as a residue from – those early days of aspiration and alienation, I have since found myself composing a revisable list of great works of literature that need to be tackled. Milton's *Paradise Lost* and Proust's *In Search of Lost Time* still summon with the disdainful nonchalance of the master work, confident they represent a forbidding climb, even with the oxygen of an annotated edition, or a critical essay or two acting as sherpas for the expedition.

Still driven, decades and careers later, by those teen South reading obsessions of my youth, I recently took on a master work of literature, Walt Whitman's *Leaves of Grass*. I believe the specific inspiration to read *Leaves of Grass* sprang from the literary backwash churned up with the 200th anniversary of his birth a few years back. Like most American high schoolers, I had read small selections of "Song of Myself" and a few recognized diadems like "When Lilacs Last in the Dooryard Bloom'd." But this was different. I meant to – and indeed scaled – all 293 poems.

There is a special experience that becomes available upon tackling a great writer's long master work. There is the sense of not merely dawdling among well-known bits and pieces but experiencing the fresh, raw encounters as one shoves off and discovers, for example, barely out of the reader's harbor, a gem like "Starting from Paumanok:" Reading it felt like a trip across the country, a walk in the factory, a descent into the mine, a drink from a cold mountain stream, a chanting of all states, States, and sexualities. As Whitman put it in the poem: "O something ecstatic and undemonstrable! O music wild! . . . haste on with me." I was off, on my long, rollicking voyage with *Leaves of Grass*.

WHITMAN'S INTENSE EMPATHY AND RADICAL INCLUSIVENESS

As I eased into *Leaves of Grass,* I noted Whitman's radical inclusiveness: "I hear America singing, the varied carols I hear," he observes in one of his famous "Inscriptions" poems that kick off his great work. In his relatively early work "Salut au Monde," he opens with an emphasis on geographic diversity that widens out to include cultural and religious diversity:

I hear the Coptic refrain toward sundown. . .
I hear the Arab muezzin calling from the top of the mosque,
I hear the Christian priests at the altars of their churches. . .
I hear the Hebrew reading his records and psalms. . ." (Section 3)

Whitman includes in his celebration of inclusiveness his own radical identification with the diverse, including "convicts and prostitutes" and other examples that in his day stood for the outcast or marginalized. "I feel I am of them," the poet notes in "You Felons on Trial in Courts." At one point in "Song of Myself" he declares he is the "witch burnt with dry wood" and "the hounded slave. . ." (Section 33).

Reading the entire work also provided glimpses of the sources – for Whitman – of this radical inclusiveness, among them, compassion and intense empathy, a robust embrace of his own boundary-crossing, expansive sense of identity, and a need to break free of stale convention, which he describes variously as "limits and imaginary / lines" ("Song of the Open Road," Section 5) and "a puny and pious life", in "A Song of Joys." He calls instead for a spirit of adventure, openness, and exploration, and for "all deeds, promiscuously done / at all times" ("Our Old Feuillage"). Whitman's inclusiveness is illustrated, formally, by his repeated cataloguing of objects, vocations, places, religions, and dozens more taxonomies.

EMBRACING POLARIZATION AND DIVISIONS OF HIS DAY

Whitman also makes clear that, poetically, at least, he accepts all that life throws his way:

I have the idea of all, and am all, and believe in all. . .
I assert that all past days were what they must have been. . .
And that to-day is what it must be. . . ("With Antecedents," Section 2)

With Whitman, there is no attempt to deny or cancel the presence of evil, traces of bad action or words, or divisions among people. Earlier in the poem, he observes that ". . . we stand amid / evil and good, / All swings around us. . . " and makes clear his effort, not to deny or try to efface but to absorb and reflect, the disputes and rancor of the "vehement days" he lived through, prior to, during and after the Civil War. In "To Him That Was Crucified" the poet elaborates on this need to confront and embrace the controversies and divisions of the polarized times one lives in:

We walk silent among the disputes and assertions, but reject not
the disputers nor anything that is asserted,
We hear the bawling and din, we are reach'd at by divisions,
jealousies, recriminations on every side. . .
Yet we walk unheld, free. . .

I was reminded of our own vehement times and found reassuring Whitman's confident embrace of a brawling, roiling marketplace of ideas, where the good ones get traction and long-term purchase and the crummy, threadbare conspiracy theories and hate mongering falter and are swept into the early morning sewers before another day in the market.

FULL CREDIT FOR SCALING MOUNT WHITMAN

As I started my own catalogue charting my responses to reading Whitman and began as well to sense Whitman's themes of inclusiveness and diversity, it was not all sunshine and reading progress. In my notes – and memories – of my months-long reading journey with Whitman, there were some dead spots. In more than one instance, I lost patience with his poetry – for example, its occasional dollops of half-digested, Emersonian-infused hocus pocus. I also sensed as I read his great work, as others have, a certain unevenness in his voluminous output. The latter third of LG seemed to sag a bit and the autumnal work of the two annexes that round it out did not seem as vital or fresh as the earlier master works and great supporting pieces.

Near the end of *LG* I found myself making tough decisions about whether I would include the secondary peaks of *Poems Excluded from Leaves of Grass* and *Uncollected Poems*, along with other excursions the editor offered. I said yes to the two annexes "Sands at Seventy" and "Goodbye My Fancy" as well as the retrospective essay "A Backward Glance O'er Travel'd Roads, the sections that round out the final 1891-92 edition, recognizing that full credit for scaling Mount Whitman required getting to the top of that "death-bed edition." I left the secondary peaks of excluded works and fragments to the Whitman scholars. I did go back and read Whitman's 1855 Preface to the first edition of *Leaves of Grass,* and then called it, well, a climb. I planted my flag of notes and musings and began the descent to the base camp of early 21st century suburbia, family, and media caterwauling.

There were times, as I imagine there usually are for others in tackling a long, master work of literature, when I felt I was reading somewhat rotely, perhaps overly focused on trying to hit some imaginary quota of pages to keep up the forward momentum in the great read. Sometimes when the sheer volume of the enterprise was overwhelming, I wondered if I would be better off just selecting (or relying on critical consensus to select) a limited number of Whitman's best poems in LG, to helicopter to the crest of the Whitman experience rather than hiking through the entire volume.

Maybe. But I'm doing something different, I told myself. This was a marathon and it had its own pleasures. I had the pleasure of a cross-country journey that enabled the discovery of little nuggets of Whitman verse – samplings that almost certainly would not have been included in any curated selections I might have read. In addition, reading a master work, in its entirety, allows you to get a good sense – the best sense you the reader are able to get – of a great artist like Whitman developing, sensing his poetic mission, his gathering power, and, for Whitman at least, registering the neglect by readers and critics of his day that so weighed on him.

CATALOGUING – AND CAREFULLY WEIGHING – WHITMAN'S NOTIONS OF EQUALITY

As I continued my journey with Whitman, I developed an urge, matching his, to catalogue some of the related themes I found coalescing around his notions of inclusiveness and identity. I found Whitman regularly celebrating a radical equality, whether male-female or black-white, standing in for broader notions of equality. As the poet put it, regarding gender equality: "And I will show you of male and female that either is but the equal of the other." ("Starting From Paumanok," Section 12). He also took issue with any notion of zero summing efforts regarding equality: ". . . as if it harm'd me, giving others the same / chances and rights as myself—as if it were not indispensable to my own rights. . ." ("Thought" *Of Equality*).

Whitman's embrace of equality between blacks and whites informs and is informed by his longstanding abolitionist opposition to slavery. The two notions edge together in "Salut Au Monde" where he celebrates "[You] black, divine-soul'd African, large, fine-headed, nobly form'd, superbly destin'd, on equal terms with me!" (Section 11). He makes clear in "Song of the Broad-Axe" that a great civilization is not where the tall buildings stand but "where the slave ceases, and the master of the slave ceases . . . There the great city stands." (Section 5). His most powerful, recurring symbol in the work, leaves of grass, he sees as

... a universal hieroglyphic
And it means, Sprouting alike in broad zones and narrow zones
Growing among black folks as among white. . .
I give them the same,
I receive them the same. ("Song of Myself," Section 6)

Whitman also illuminates – and feels – the deforming role that a powerful nation like the United States, or a powerful race or section of the country at a pivotal moment, can have in entrenching injustice and on efforts for equality between people:

I see the enslaved, the overthrown, the hurt, the opprest of the
    whole earth,
I feel the measureless shame and humiliation of my race, it
becomes all mine. . . " ("The Mystic Trumpeter," Section 7).

This view serves as a useful corrective to some of the poet's over-the-top poetic celebrations of America that, in places in the early work, occasionally slide into a type of jingoistic embrace of America. It is also important to note Whitman the man was no plaster saint. A tiny sampling I made of articles related to Whitman's racial attitudes turned up some examples of casual racism, in his broader writings and statements, showing, as with Lincoln and great abolitionists like William Lloyd Garrison, racial attitudes of the day had their impact. One recent critic, Lavelle Porter, noting some of the problematic references, even posed the question, "Should Whitman Be #Cancelled?" Scholar Ed Folsom noted, in the same article, "the temptation to talk back to Walt Whitman has always been great. . ." while placing the emphasis, like Porter, on continued engagement with the writer.

GIVING VOICE TO DIVERSITY AND DIFFERENCE

At moments in *Leaves of Grass*, the poet cites and gently celebrates John Brown, the great but violent abolitionist eventually executed for the raid he led on the federal arsenal at Harper's Ferry: "I would sing how an old man, tall, with white hair, mounted / the scaffold in Virginia. ("Year of Meteors"). Also merging with Whitman's celebration of equality and proud advocacy of the abolitionist cause is his embrace in "Song of Myself" of the voiceless and dispossessed:

>Through me many long, dumb voices,
>Voices of the interminable generations of prisoners and slaves,
>Voices of the diseas'd and despairing... (Section 24)

Whitman not only celebrated diversity, but the importance of rejecting unexamined tradition, as well as old "creeds" and "others' formulas" ("Song of the Redwood Tree"). The poet emphasizes his comfort with "paths untrodden, / In the growth by the margins... [Away] From all the standards hitherto publish'd..." ("In Paths Untrodden").

In poems like "In Paths Untrodden" (and throughout the Calamus section of Leaves of Grass in which it appears, and elsewhere), Whitman makes clear that his celebration of diversity and difference, and his embrace of transgressive identity revolve to a significant degree around his resolution "to sing no songs to-day but those of manly attachment". His is a poetry, a fervent, alternately open, and coded, embrace of homosexuality, of gay and queer yearnings and experiences:

>I proceed for all who are or have been young men,
>To tell the secrets of my nights and days,
>To celebrate the needs of comrades.

In "This Moment Yearning and Thoughtful," the poet sees "men in other lands yearning / and thoughtful... O I know we should be brethren and lovers. . . ." The speaker in one poem emphasizes that regardless of whatever successes life brought, whether personal or artistic, they did not bring happiness. But "when I thought how my dear friend my lover was on his / way coming, O then I was happy." ("When I Heard at the Close of Day").

While Whitman on occasion made statements to friends or

correspondents denying his homosexuality and any male-homoerotic
sentiment in his poetry (his exchange with the poet John Addington
Symonds providing one well-known example), the impulse in his poetry
is clear, coding and all, and it fits within his broader championing of
diversity, equality, and identity, his celebration of "the flesh and the
appetites," and his commingling of the flesh, desire, and identity: "Is
this then a touch? quivering me to a new identity . . . " He points to his
mission to liberate transgressive identity: "Through me forbidden voices,/
Voices of sexes and lusts, voices veil'd and I remove the veil. . . ." ("Song
of Myself," Sections 28, 24).

AWAKE AMONG THE SLEEPWALKERS
    In this great summons to diversity and difference that is Leaves
of Grass, Whitman sees himself as 'woke,' perhaps the first great woke
writer in America, and summons the reader to identify, as I read him
in this early 21st century timeframe, as the opposite of those who
sleepwalk their way through life and "go toward false realities" and "pass
unwittingly the true realities of life . . . " In the same poem, trotting out
a French term for sleepwalkers, the poet makes clear, by implication, his
'wokeness' in describing the unwoke: "And often to me they are sad, hasty
unwaked sonnambules / walking in the dusk. . ." ("Thought" *of persons
arrived at high positions*). In "The Sleepers," a more difficult, complex
poem, the poet picks up a version of this sleeping/'woke' opposition
and contrasts his aware, visionary, active state – a consciousness awake
to empathy, political concern, and openness to sexual/male-homoerotic
experience – to those sleeping, without such awareness or experience:
    I wander all night in my vision. . .
    Bending with open eyes over the shut eyes of sleepers. . .
    I stand in the dark with drooping eyes by the worst suffering. . .
    The restless sink in their beds, they fitfully sleep.

AMERICA'S TURBULENT DEMOCRACY
    It is interesting to note that for Whitman, being woke to realities
in his day broadened out and embraced an appreciation and a concern

for democracy. Whitman in LG sees America as experimental and improvisational, but also representing the culminating ideal of governance, with its rule by common citizens in a land not haunted by "the ghosts of uncrown'd ladies [and] rejected kings." ("Song of the Broad-Axe"). At the same time Whitman acknowledges that American democracy "will always be agitated and turbulent," with Americans hostage to "the terrible significance of their elections." ("Prefatory Letter to Ralph Waldo Emerson"; "Preface 1855—*Leaves of Grass*, First Edition").

THE GREAT 'AWOKENING': RESPONSIBILITIES FOR THE READER

The Whitman summons to wokeness includes responsibilities for the reader: the poet sees his poetry as an invitation to dialogue and a call to action: "The reader will always have his or her part to do, just as much as I have had mine," he observes in his wonderful valedictory essay, "A Backward Glance O'er Travel'd Roads." He urges readers, later in the same piece ,"to pursue your own flight" and "be lifted into a different light and atmosphere."

I acknowledge two related truths in embracing the term 'woke' to evoke a coherent Whitman vision in his poetry: first, a truism, that of course Whitman's mid- and late 19th century America is very different from our own and whatever he invoked, prophesied, celebrated, or transgressed were mere seeds, or, put another way, anticipatory soundings, of what these attitudes have come to signify today. But what powerful, shaping messages they were, even with the blemishes some critics have noted. And second, that 'woke' is an immensely fertile notion, with a long, proud lineage in the Black community. References to it date back as far as 1938, when blues singer Huddie William Ledbetter (performing as Lead Belly) in a spoken afterword to his song about the Scottsboro Boys, urged Blacks to "stay woke" to the dangers they faced in a racist, Jim Crow America. Fast forward, since the 2014 killing of Michael Brown in Ferguson, Missouri, and subsequent similar incidents, the term has also come to signal the need for vigilance about police brutality and racial discrimination and profiling. On a parallel track, notions of woke in the 1980s (and earlier in some instances) broke out of the black community and began service in the broader culture, while also prompting, more recently, an eventual conservative backlash. That a powerful, reactionary political faction in our time would seek to subvert and weaponize this useful, storied construct – in order to call into question explorations and celebrations of diversity, equality, inclusion, and transgressive identity – would not have surprised Whitman.

As I concluded my extended journey with Whitman, including a sustained return-to-base camp review of my sprawling notes, a sense of what I had taken from the poet – what I wanted to take – awoke within me. I wondered if I had the right to ignore 17-plus decades of criticism – articles and books numbering in the tens of thousands, and still proliferating – and most of the available biographical information, beyond the distilled, informed sampling the editor offered me. And invoking my rights as a reader, I answered in the affirmative.

I also wondered sometimes if I was guilty of readerly cherry picking: Do I have the right to do my own cataloguing of lines and themes, to emphasize what was important to me, as a reader? My aspiration in putting together my little taxonomy is to have remained faithful to Whitman's admonition to the reader: "I charge you forever reject those who would expound me" and his related call to his reader "I charge that there be no theory or school founded out of me." ("Myself and Mine").

But in the end, Whitman wanted readers, plain old readers, in some respects like him, the highly motivated autodidact whose formal schooling amounted to little more than six years in his youth (even as he read voraciously and educated himself the rest of his life). As he put it in the same poem, he wanted readers who would read and engage with the poetry and take him at his word, not, through "the accounts of my friends." He understood that Leaves of Grass would be challenging for readers to understand and embrace.

Given his focus on active readers, I like to think Whitman would accept my humble taxonomy, the testimony of one reader, awake to the possibilities of interpretation – my interpretation and appreciation of his poetry – as I sought to take its measure. And I believe he might have nodded in assent to my modest catalogue of wokeness I have claimed to discern in this magnificent collection of poems. For, as with any reading experience and account, it is a testimony, a narrative of impact and response, and an attempt – in this early 21st century timeframe – to order that response in a manner that respects Whitman's original – and deepest – intentions. To take the measure of the poetry, to assess and appreciate the scale of the achievement, for his time and ours, this is what we readers do.

WHAT SMALL BIRDS DO

Once I held in my hand a yellow finch –
it hopped through the front yard, escaped or
turned out pet. It trembled to vibration
against my palm, strong heartbeat I took for frailty.

My grandma loved the little birds, thought them
more deserving of the feeder's seeds, bullied by blue jays
and cold winds. Divorced young, with four daughters,
did she see herself in feathers puffed against winter?

A Western bluebird, tattoo memorial, rides
my shoulder, gripping a flowering branch, head
turned, eye alert, beak about to open in his *cheer-che-cheer* call.
A friend to gardeners everywhere, one web site describes.

When my cousin and I were toddlers,
Grandma planted us a garden in her side yard.
A small meadow of violets and alyssum,
Purple and white carpet that we stepped on eagerly.

When we crouched down and began to pull up flowers,
our mothers rushed to stop us. *It's their garden,*
Grandma insisted. *Whatever they do is fine.*
Her garden always a master class in color and texture:

ferns and roses, lemon tree and bird of paradise,
camellias and begonias, cypress and pepper tree.

She gave me a stretch of flowerbed for my own first garden:
nasturtiums and delphinium, cosmos and alyssum,

flowers that still mean refuge when the world turns
cold. I still sometimes must make my own warmth,
feel my heart beat wildly against the unfamiliar, listen
for my bluebird to sing *cheer-che-cheer.*

MAPLE

I wonder why I've not been
writing   is it because
I've been feeling so tired
as now   almost midnight
I don't know how
to keep going
or what will come next
There's still the challenge
and loneliness   as the tree
at the end of our street
keeps its leaves
through November
I don't know the name
for such a red   pale or
rich as the leaves turn
with blue and yellow
in the layers of hue
Everyone is noticing the tree
and speaks to me of it
Myron texted
a picture   *Have you seen*
this tree?   Myron whom I
don't know well   nor did I know
his wife well   but there was
love between us   feelings
expressed   and so I keep
her —   the many times

we came upon each other
in the garden-store or
passing through
the square   and stood a long
time together   engrossed
by whatever was happening
perennials   aging   our children
what we dreamed
of making   or becoming
She took *Winter Roses* with her
to the hospital one time
and told me later my poems
were company
I missed my chance to see
her   a few summers ago
I kept putting it off
like the writing   I say I'll
do it later
Marian is gone but Myron
is still here   and he said I
was a good friend to his
wife   brushing aside my
worry
So   that he shares the tree's
beauty with me
means something important
Even now   this very second
there's the tree

ENDURANCE

WHEN we were nineteen, Makenna Solomon was my best friend. She did all the things I thought best friends should do: she told me secrets, she lay in bed with me while we watched reality TV marathons on her laptop, she organized trips to Costco and always offered to split the cost of that 96-count box of Tampax. We were both competitive, but in a friendly way; we never fought over anything important, never boys or coursework or anything like that. It was small stuff, like how she borrowed my nail polish without asking, or how I called her rich when she thought of herself as middle class. Or how we played Settlers of Catan with a group of friends, and when she won, I accused her of cheating, and she told me I was a loser, that I'd always be a loser, and we didn't talk for a week. But she also took care of me the way an older sister would. Whenever she heard me crying in my room at night, she'd come in and turn me into a burrito, tucking me under my comforter so tight that I couldn't move my legs, and I'd end up laughing at the ridiculousness of it all, and she'd pat me on the forehead and tell me to have sweet dreams.

Now, ten years later, she owns a *Survivor*-themed "brew works and entertainment business" called Endurance, Inc., and I work for her. I'm a glorified server—the term she uses is "Challenge Host"—and I've been here for over a year now, no end in sight. In fact, I'm currently holding a covered tray, staring up at a group of women in their early twenties who booked Endurance, Inc. for a bachelorette party. They're hanging upside-down from a horizontal wooden pole, like pigs roasting on a spit.

I hope they're in pain.

I adjust my mask, clear my throat, and chirp a line from the "approved scripts" section of the Employee Handbook: "Maybe I can tempt you. The first two competitors to quit will get to share this." I lift the cover from my tray with a flourish and reveal a Mudslide in an enormous curved glass, piled with whipped cream and chocolate sprinkles, light on the Kahlua (but they don't know that). At this point in my life, I think it looks disgusting, like hours of indigestion, but the women groan with longing, as most of our customers do. They're only a few years younger than me, but it feels like a lifetime separates us.

Their faces look deflated and red from this angle. They aren't required to wear masks when they're doing a challenge, which makes me uncomfortable; I'm convinced that hanging upside-down like this could cause any number of weird bodily secretions. They look like Troll dolls, hair floating above their heads.

"I hate you, Katrina!" one of them shrieks at the bride-to-be.

"Oh, shut up," the bride responds happily, her face a scary shade of purple.

Another member of the party says, "I wasn't going to win anyway," and swings her feet down, hanging for a second from her fingertips. Then she tumbles a few feet into the sand below and tries to regain her balance. For a moment, she wears that same blank expression I've seen so many times, the one people make when their vision momentarily fades to black. Then the blood rushes back into her face and she blinks—and just like that, she's totally fine.

She marches triumphantly over to me and snatches the glass from my tray.

"If no one else drops, do I get to drink this all by myself?" she asks loudly, clearly trying to entice one of her friends to join her.

"You sure do," I say, aware of my fake-sounding tone but unable to change it. "Any other takers?" I call, but one of them just flips me the finger before readjusting on the pole.

Seven women remain in the challenge, which is an Endurance, Inc. favorite. We call it Hold on Loosely (But Don't Let Go). Most of our customers give up after a few minutes, especially the bachelorette parties, and then they move on to the next challenge. There are five challenges in total, and you get a discount rate if your party wants to do all five.

Unfortunately for me, Makenna doesn't pay by the hour; rather, I get a flat rate upfront, and then it's up to me to "tempt" the customers to give up so I can take my money and go home. If the bachelorettes want to hang on that pole all night, there's not much I can do to stop them.

The woman who just lost the challenge grabs a spoon and swills it around in the whipped cream, then takes a long, self-satisfied lick. "Y'all are dumb!" she yells at her friends.

Or maybe they're being reasonable for not wanting to share drinks during a pandemic. Who's to say?

The Mudslide and anything else I bring out as a "temptation" is added to the group's bill, of course. This particular business practice has inspired a few tense moments in the past—most of our customers seem to think that the temptations are part of the initial fee, rather than an added expense—and I've told Makenna she should make this clearer in the Terms & Conditions, but she doesn't want to lose out on the extra income.

Turns out, opening a business at the beginning of a pandemic is kind of a bad idea.

"It's such a unique business, though," Makenna will say on days when we're the only two people here, when we sit together at the registration desk and stare at the empty sidewalk outside. As if being unique should exempt her from financial hardship.

The radio on my belt beeps. I trudge through the sand that covers the floor, away from the bachelorette party, trying to get a bit of distance before radioing Makenna in return. A monkey howls over the speaker at the corner of the ceiling—the only music we play here is jungle-themed—and I wait for it to stop.

"Yes?" I finally ask, quietly, into the radio. I hate the idea of a customer overhearing. It's embarrassing, sometimes, the way Makenna talks to me.

"Why are there still seven customers hanging on the spit?" she asks. "It's been fifteen minutes."

"Maybe they do Crossfit in their free time?" I answer. "Or they all play on their college volleyball team?"

"Why aren't you trying to get them down?"

I look towards the glass wall that divides the challenge room from the bar, but I can't see her in the shadows. This space used to be a gymnastics gym; all the helicopter parents sat behind that glass wall and watched their kids on the balance beam, the floor, the trampoline. That's all gone now. The entire floor is covered with sand. The bar, out there, is tiki-themed.

"Are you not feeling well?" Makenna presses over the radio. "Do you need to rest?"

She loves to talk about my health. An enduring habit from college. "I'm fine."

"Then why have you only offered one temptation?"

"No one cares about temptations," I say, starting an old argument. "It's not like on *Survivor,* where people literally eat one scoop of rice per day and will do anything for a cookie."

"If you have a better idea, please enlighten me."

I can picture her tugging on one of the dark curls that frames her face, her lips pressed together in a way that makes her fair skin look wrinkled. But she doesn't want to hear my ideas; I figured that out a long time ago. Endurance, Inc. is her baby.

Even though the whole business was my idea.

When Makenna and I were roommates, I had to take a semester off— dean's orders—and all I did was watch TV. I torrented all the old *Survivor* seasons and watched them back-to-back. Makenna was still pre-med at the time, so her course schedule was rough, but she always got sucked into the show while she was meant to be doing problem sets. I'd prop my laptop on a couch cushion, and she'd curl up beside me, a textbook open on the couch at her feet.

One day, we were watching the *Survivor* contestants participate in an immunity challenge. They stood in a row, their wrists attached to buckets of water suspended over their heads. If they let their hands fall even the tiniest bit, the water would come pouring down.

"I bet I could beat all of them," Makenna said off-handedly.

She wasn't much more athletic than me, but she had a habit of soliloquizing about how she was on a State Championship-winning track and field team in high school. She knew I didn't play sports or work out.

Before that semester, I'd never had the time, always squeezing in part-time jobs around my course schedule.

I said something like, "It's probably a lot harder than it looks."

She made a dismissive sound. On screen, one of the contestants let his hand drop. Water cascaded over his head and shoulders.

It would be interesting, I thought, to see who would win. Makenna or me. Everything in her life had always been so easy. I was the one who knew the meaning of hard work.

"Wouldn't it be cool," I said, "if there were a place where you could actually try some of these endurance challenges? Without having to go on the show, I mean."

"You mean a gym?" she asked, teasing.

"Gyms don't have that kind of thing," I said defensively, even though I couldn't be sure. "It would be like one of those places that has paintball or ropes courses. A specialty place for birthday parties and big groups. Tired of bowling? Try endurance challenges instead!"

She made an unimpressed little noise in the back of her throat.

Makenna graduated before I did. She always said she'd stay in Madison for a while until she figured out what she wanted to do—she abandoned all hopes of being a doctor sometime around the end of her junior year—but then she took a consulting job in Chicago, and she left me to find a subletter. I didn't try to make her stay. I figured I'd probably been enough of a burden to her over the years.

When I finally graduated, I found an apartment a few streets down from the one Makenna and I used to share on Few Street. We kept in touch, but our phone calls grew farther and farther apart. She launched a bespoke sock company that failed. Then she dabbled in LuLaRoe. I lost track of her around that time. She sent me a text that said something like, "Hey, I recently found a great way to make some passive income! Would you be open to additional revenue streams?"

I didn't respond. I had realized that my life always went on, whether or not Makenna was in it.

Then, about two years ago, she showed up in Madison for an alumni networking event—she'd gotten married, and her husband wanted to move back—and we reconnected. Or, I should say, she reconnected with me. I didn't go out of my way to get back into her good graces, but she texted me constantly, left rambling voice memos. It quickly became clear that she had become *that kind* of person, the kind who latched on. I recognized the type because that's who I used to be. Needy. Lonely. I saw my old self in her, and I hated it.

I didn't have much say in our renewed friendship. But even when we were in college, that's how we functioned. She came up with the plans, she set the expectations. Back then, I loved this about her. Like, she used to mail me a box of gifts every Christmas. No one ever gave me that many gifts, especially not my dad, who buried himself so deeply into the couch at home, Sports Center blaring at all hours, that he seemed to forget the holidays completely. I loved Makenna's gifts, but every Christmas I went into a panic, searching desperately for something meaningful to send her that wouldn't cost more than twenty dollars. I usually ended up making her a gift—a friendship bracelet, a sad crocheted frog for her desk—and she would call me and say something kind, like, "Thanks, hun. I love it so much," and then I'd never see the thing again, never on her wrist, never on her desk.

Anyway, after she moved back to Madison, we started getting dinner once a week. She often called me during the workday, when she was bored or driving home from the yoga class her husband paid for. I always put her on speaker and set my phone on a high shelf, continuing to answer emails while she talked. Ever since I was twenty-four I worked as a remote customer service employee for a rideshare app. It wasn't glamorous, but the pay was decent. It was unclear whether Makenna knew what I did for work; she rarely asked about it.

One day she called me like she always did, and she said, "I'm starting a new business. You're going to love it." That's how she opened the phone call—no hi, how have you been, sorry to interrupt your day.

She went on to describe everything she had accomplished already: she had signed a commercial lease for the warehouse, found a builder for the endurance challenges, worked with a lawyer to finalize the liability waivers, obtained the liquor license, strategized a marketing campaign.

"Wait. Endurance challenges?" I asked, clicking send on another *No, you can't have a refund* email as my brain caught up to the conversation.

"Yes, endurance challenges. Did you not hear me describe the company?"

"Sorry, I got distracted. Say it again?"

"I'm opening a *Survivor*-themed company. I'm calling it a 'bar and entertainment business.' Or maybe 'brew works' is better. There'll be beer, but I'm sure as hell not brewing it."

I felt something close in my chest, like a door snapped shut by a mysterious draft.

I didn't have the nerve to say it like an accusation, so the words came out lilting, teasing: "Wasn't that my idea?" It was the same joking tone we used in college: *God, bitch, did you really just do that*?

She laughed. "It was my idea, remember? We were on the couch in our old living room, and a lightbulb went off in my head, and you said it'd never work. But you did inspire me. You're the one who got me hooked on *Survivor* in the first place."

She chattered happily for a few more minutes, saying that her husband was helping her with the startup costs, that he was thrilled for her to go out on a limb and try being an entrepreneur again.

When she finally hung up, I threw my phone across the room, breaking the screen in two places, and then I called my therapist, feeling the micro abrasions in the glass catching on the pad of my thumb as I dialed.

THE grand opening of Endurance, Inc. was scheduled for Thursday, March 12, 2020. That same day, the governor of Wisconsin declared a state of emergency. The opening got postponed once, twice, three times.

Privately, I thought this was some sort of karmic revenge because Makenna had stolen my idea. I felt gleeful every time she texted me to say that the opening had been delayed. But then I got laid off, and my health insurance evaporated. I had an ungodly amount of debt. My savings were embarrassingly meager.

I knew Makenna needed employees as much as I needed a job. There weren't many people in Madison that spring who were eager to work indoors, in-person, for a brand-new, likely-to-fail company that no one had ever heard of. But even so, when she asked me to be a Challenge Host, she did so with a pitying look in her eyes, an implication that she was doing this out of the goodness of her heart. "I know how hard things have been for you," she said

My breath caught in my lungs. I wanted to refuse, to spit, to tell her I had been doing fine, just fine, for so very many years without her.

But on June 5, 2020, Makenna cut the ribbon, even though the county's emergency order meant that she could only open at 25 percent capacity. Just a week before, Wisconsin had a record-breaking 733 COVID cases reported in just one day.

I hung my head, donned my cloth mask, and went to work.

I MENTIONED there are five challenges to choose from at Endurance, Inc., but we started with only two: Hold on Loosely (But Don't Let Go) and Tree Hugger. We hardly had any business, those first few months, and then in November of 2020 all indoor gatherings were banned, and Makenna temporarily shuttered our doors for the holiday season. She didn't stop planning, though, and by February 2021, she'd installed two more challenges, Hands Held High and Numb Buckets, and she reluctantly implemented my designs for a team challenge called Don't Drop the Snake.

As much as I hate to admit it, working with Makenna on Endurance, Inc. kept me going through the dark months. It gave me something to think about that wasn't just sickness, sickness, death, death. And it was nice to feel close with someone again, nice to feel like part of a team. I remembered us in college, hunkered in our apartment during the coldest days when the lakes would freeze and our windows crusted with ice.

Vaccines rolled out that spring, and finally, finally, the summer brought real business. It helped that our building had garage doors on one end, which we could open and let the fresh air roll in over the sand. We all felt safer that way. The Paint 'N' Sip across the street didn't have the same luxury, and I often saw a woman in there walking back and forth across the empty studio, cleaning the storefront window from the inside, gazing out.

The hubris of that summer inspired Makenna to implement a classic *Survivor* eating challenge, where customers raced to eat pig brains and dried cockroaches and fertilized duck eggs known as balut. It was amazing to watch strangers arrive in droves to eat bugs, to laugh with the friends they hadn't seen in months and celebrate being vaccinated while choking on giant fish eyes. But the fun only lasted a few weeks. It was hard to find locally-sourced stuff, and then the Delta-variant cropped up, and Makenna blamed me for the money we lost. She said the eating challenge was my idea, my fault, even though the two of us had dreamed it up together one night over the phone. Of course she would credit me for her failures, but never for the business itself. Never that.

At the height of our success, Makenna employed ten servers. She fired six at the end of the summer.

Now here we are, October, wearing KN-95s and cringing at our customers' open mouths, acutely aware of their breath circulating around the small tiki bar. At least I am. Makenna tries to play it off like she doesn't care, like she's not afraid of getting sick.

One Tuesday I arrive at work and find that our only registered group—a boy scout troop—has canceled at the last minute. I won't be getting paid tonight. There's no one here except Makenna, who has taken off her mask, her forehead resting on her arms atop the polished wood of the bar.

"You can go home," she says without lifting her head. "There's no one else coming."

"I assume you won't reimburse me for gas?"

I say it like I'm joking, but she makes a frustrated noise and says, "I'm hemorrhaging money here, Soph. Do you not get that?"

I sit on the stool beside her. In the old days we were the touchy-feely kind of friends, always seeking out each other's warmth.

I could place my hand between her shoulder blades, but I don't.

We sit silently for a moment, two, and then I say, "I have an idea."

She finally looks up at me, a red mark on her forehead. There's the faintest glimmer of hope in her eyes, and I wonder if she thinks I have a plan, a business idea that will make everything better. Instead I say, "Let's do Tree Hugger. Right now. Fifty bucks says I'll win."

She groans and puts her head back down. "I'm not in the mood for games."

I have never seen Makenna try any of the challenges. She always refuses when I dare her to compete with me. I suspect she's trying not to embarrass me. She's always been so sure of herself, so confident in her own superiority. She's trying to save me from myself, the way she always did.

I give her a little nudge, then run from the bar out to the open sand. I kick off my shoes and climb the ladder up to the top of Tree Hugger, then call out to Makenna, "Come on!"

The door to the bar has swung shut, but I see the shape of Makenna move to the glass wall, watching me from the shadows.

I wrap my arms around the top of the vertical wooden pole. Tree Hugger is a classic challenge. Each contestant gets their own wooden pole, about ten feet tall and a foot in diameter. There are small footholds carved into it, and you have to cling to it for as long as you can without touching the ground.

I swing my feet off the ladder and hook my legs around the pole, my bare feet clinging for purchase against the smooth wood. I feel around for a foothold but don't connect with any. I begin to slide.

"What are you afraid of?" I call out, but if Makenna replies, I don't hear it. I slide right down to the sand, landing on my butt with a painful thump.

MAKENNA surprises me the following week with an invitation to her thirtieth birthday, which she plans to host at Endurance, Inc. She has invited a few of our old college friends who still live in town, and she tells me to extend the invitation to my other friends, but I don't really have any. I don't even have former-coworker friends—a symptom of being a remote employee for so many years. When I got laid off, I shipped my laptop back and that was that.

On the night of the party, I stand at the reception desk and greet the guests. The few faces I know from college seem surprised to see me, if they recognize me at all; I've lived in town all these years but I haven't kept up with any of them.

Makenna's husband arrives by himself, wearing a navy suit that he must have worn to his law firm that morning. He runs his hand through his graying hair and glances around the room like he'd rather be anywhere else. We've met before, but he acts like we haven't. Makenna runs up to him and gives him a peck on the cheek, then takes him by the hand and drags him out into the sand, showing him all the changes we've made. As far as I know, he hasn't visited since the spring.

Makenna has paid two Challenge Hosts to walk around with trays of shots and Mai Thais, and they both glare at me when I ask for a margarita. They're seniors at UW-Madison, my alma mater, but they know I'm not someone to ask for career advice or mentorship. I have a feeling they resent me for my current station in life, nearly thirty and making the same hourly wage as them. I tug my mask down to my chin and gulp the margarita like it's water.

After everyone has had a drink or two, they want to do the challenges. They gravitate toward Tree Hugger, all those vertical poles in the sand. Makenna's husband remains at the bar, his legs crossed as he observes from a dark corner.

When Makenna says she doesn't want to play, she gives me the briefest glance, then looks away.

"Come on, birthday girl!" An old college acquaintance whose name I don't remember claps a hand on Makenna's shoulder and gives her a shake. He looks exactly the same as he did in college, a total babyface.

Makenna looks toward the bar and shakes her head. "No, thanks. I'll facilitate."

I find myself wanting to goad her, to shake her out of this mood. "You're just afraid you'll lose," I say.

The guy from college gives a long, low whistle. A few of the other guests hear and respond in kind.

I'm afraid I've angered her. She marches through the sand and kicks off her sandals at the base of one of the Tree Hugger poles. Then she theatrically rips off her mask and tosses it to the sand, and the group cheers.

I give an appreciative whoop and she catches my eye. I smile through my mask, and she raises an eyebrow and mouths the words, You asked for it.

AFTER an hour and twenty-two minutes, Makenna and I are the only two holding on. The effort has me shaking and desperate. I find myself shouting things at her, taunting her, half-joking and half-not.

"Give up already!" I cry, my forehead resting against the wood of the pole. My arms are wrapped around it and my fingers dig into the skin just above my elbows, clenching so hard that even my knuckles have gone white. My mask is making it hard to breathe, and I know that any second now I'm going to lose my grip and slide all the way to the sand.

"I will not," she hisses. Her thighs quake with effort.

"I'm stronger than you!"

"You have never been stronger than me!"

I have a good view of the giant digital timer, which moves so slowly I swear it's malfunctioning. The party guests are clustered in groups below us, drinking and chatting and generally forgetting that Makenna and I are in a battle of epic proportions right above them.

My left toe slips and my stomach drops—I'm sliding—but then I catch myself on the next foothold, a few feet below the first. "Why won't you ever let me win?" I sound like a whiny child. I suddenly remember saying this exact phrase that night in college when we played Catan, when she called me a loser.

She makes a frustrated noise and I peer over my arm at her as she tries to readjust, her toes slipping against the pole.

My fingers are numb, but I can't unclench them. "You win at everything," I say. "All the time."

She laughs grimly at that. "I guess you haven't noticed that this business is a massive failure."

"It's not."

"It is. Eric wants me to close. He says I've wasted his money."

I glance down at the party below, but no one is paying attention to us. I can't see her husband but I'm suddenly sure he's watching. Assessing.

I feel tears starting at the corners of my eyes and I don't know why. I don't know if I'm mad at her for not telling me about this, or if I'm mad at her husband for controlling her, or if I'm mad at myself for being mad, for being a part of this mess to begin with. It's none of my business.

This is not my business.

I close my eyes and picture us, Makenna and me, back when everything was simple. Late-night hangouts at the Memorial Union, watching the boats out on the lake and drinking Spotted Cow by the pitcher. Racing each other on our bikes, following the bike path through town all the way to our shared apartment, my feet pumping on the pedals.

Then I'm on the couch in our shared living room, curled on my side. My mother died weeks ago, or months ago—it's all the same, it never gets better—and Makenna is here, her arm hugging my waist. She has made me peppermint tea. She also brought me Chippy, the purple squirrel I've had since I was two and which I usually keep hidden in my underwear drawer. *Survivor* plays on my laptop, though I'm hardly watching.

Even though she has so much studying to do tonight, she stays here for a long time. During one of those moments where I feel empty of tears, empty of any feeling at all, she brings up that old idea again, the one about the *Survivor* business with endurance challenges for anyone to try. She paints me a picture of how it could work, and I cling to the sound of her voice, this ridiculous vision of the future.

And she says, *We could run the whole thing together.*

I open my eyes. Makenna is shaking, holding on with all her might. "You can't close," I say, my voice breaking halfway through the sentence.

Our eyes meet, and I remember the day she visited me at the hospital, the white room, her pockets empty. She was about to graduate. I still had months, years, to go. I never thought I'd make it.

She only visited that one time. But she's here now, and so am I.

I will not fall. I will breathe into the pain. I will take this one moment at a time, minute by minute, hour by hour, because I can't bear the thought of letting go.

INDUSTRIAL, MIXED USE

Parcel # 179-183-16 contains 10,454 Sq. Ft. and was built in 1979

You have grabbed the last wrench from the box,
hoses loose, grease oozing from o-rings,
chisels & drivers nicked with engine gore.
You can only replace an impeller so many times
before the rubber blades no longer push water,
before the cylinders start coughing up blue smoke,
& you possess an oil pan so gritted
not even degreaser has the patience
to clean it anymore. When we were kids,
we used to dip our hands in the solvent tank,
inhale the fumes until our eyes turned
as red as a check engine light.
We have swept oil sand from the chipped
gray-painted shop floor more times
than you can count on an odometer,
totaled up the bolts in an inventory box
more times than the swipe of a credit card
at the cash register. We wanted to impress
the geriatric mechanics–those guys
with oversized paychecks & steel washers
pushed over their wedding fingers.
We'd envy their enjoyment of a workday Lucky Lager
in blue coveralls that disguised heavy metal
T-shirts, masked work order ink blots & sweat.
Fifty summers of oil stains on gravel built

a lifetime. Now they are gone & we are gone
& the workbench sits as empty as a weekend gas tank.
All those tools lined up in boxes,
chances to choose, to see what would become,
now lie like coffined bodies.

TENDER YEARS: A BRIEF MEMOIR WITH "EDDIE AND THE CRUISERS"

A season by its weather swaps our footwear
and our garments as we travel snow-swept roads
without volition. This is what it means to tremolo
and slide. Nobody lives up to their memoirs;
no story can remain accurate once it's set down.
Call it the always-evanescent present, call it
time passed before it's arrived, call it self-mythology,
the putrefying masque of the persona, tail lights
tailing off in epistrophe—call this carnelian,
collodion of nightfall—young John, dumb bag
of bones riding that stretch of Ike's interstate
between Allen Park and Marshall in his parents'
Escort wagon—call it an exculpatory metaphor
for how the self is interpellated a priori by
an ideological interstate apparatus, call it a parody
of Althusser, call it a staid middle class epistle.
He lies on the backseat, the chairs collapsed,
and watches *Eddie and the Cruisers* on a 12"
TV/VCR combo plugged into the cigarette lighter
while herds of deer peek out of weeds in roadside culverts—
call it distantiation of the self from self, palinode
of an early maunder. Pale as moonlight, skinny
as a wicket John, bag of bones, and why
was that film made, and why was he watching it
on his way past shelterbelts and maize fields turned

the blue of dusk, late autumn, single stoplight towns
with gas stations and landbound kettle lakes
and porn shops advertising "live peep shows"
and party stores advertising "live night crawlers."
Call it the vomitous underbelly of the rural idyll
or something pithier than that if you think of it.
He learns the word "caesura," he learns the name
"Rimbaud," learns the anaphora of anaphora of songs—
that a life is a set of cylindrical structures for those
beyond us to decode. In the film the music's mostly diegetic—
Chevy Bel Air dangling from the Raritan Bridge
in the morning rain while "Wild Summer Nights"
implausibly plays on its radio. In a classroom in Ocean City,
Frank Ridgeway (Tom Berenger), the bandmember
they called "The Word Man," is puzzling over
"Lines Composed a Few Miles Above Tintern Abbey"
while flashing back to a moment playing "Tender Years"
on a baby grand on some bandstand in Atlantic City,
and is this diegetic, happening as it does twenty years remote
from the empty classroom where he dreams? Call it
the polemic against music in real time, call it the irrefutable
oneiric quality of song. Every poem is a persona poem,
a friend will tell our passenger many years later, and if this is true,
every poem is a palinode of a self worn down to its seams
in ventriloquy and maunder, which means we'll never know
who Eddie Wilson or Arthur Rimbaud really were while knowing
that no one really is anyone once the credits roll.
John Cafferty's soundtrack was criticized for its anachrony
(the band was from the early 60s but Cafferty sounded
like 80s Springsteen). *Do people change or don't they,*
that's what Wordsworth's getting at, Ridgeway says.
For the longest time he heard it as "words worth getting at,"
not an author name but a question of emphasis—anaphora,

epistrophe, refrain. When Eddie Wilson comes back,
a reflection watching his younger self in a cathode ray tube
TV in the display front of an appliance store, his ensuing visitations
to former band members offer an answer our passenger holds onto
hopelessly. Call it stumbling the parapets of before,
the putative before. A man watches himself watching his former self,
a Bel Air from a bridge rail, every poem is a persona poem
just as every resurrection, every film, every happy accident
involves some improbable possibility—a recovered
reel-to-reel, a missing stone, a living ghost.

BOULDER BLUES

WE sat near the continental air access tunnel. My father wore a Lilly Daché button-up, khaki pants, and blue joggers. Daddyo was upset that my mother and Jen were visiting the airport gift shop. He thought shopping was a distraction and they'd miss our departure to Denver.

Troy leaned against a cement pillar with his arms crossed. He looked away when our eyes met. I knew he'd come only for appearances. He felt I was our father's favored son. But he was his own favorite child, a force of nature who'd beaten incredible odds to become a success.

My father checked his Timex. He removed his glasses and slipped them back on. He stuck a hand in his pocket and jiggled the change. He re-checked his wristwatch.

My mother had returned a week early to bid me farewell. During her Boston sojourn, she'd discovered a hip Coolidge Corner salon and returned with Jane Fonda's gypsy shag. Passing pilots had tipped their hats. Her eyes burned with a renewed vitality and I suspected she'd romped like a teenager through Boston. Troy had told me Fletcher treated her to dinner and drinks at the Black Rose Tavern. Jen had filled me in on Gert's chief concerns, including reminding our mother that a tiny Commonwealth Avenue apartment "couldn't hold a candle to" a sprawling Kahala ranch house. Her flat was furnished with the melancholy remnants of her former life as a stock broker's wife. The dining room boasted Baroque end tables and a blue velvet divan. A gold art nouveau chandelier lit a mahogany table for twelve. Serpentine dressers jazzed up the bedrooms and an art deco mirror hung by wires off the pantry wall. A red baby grand gathered dust below a window sealed shut by mold. The apartment must have haunted my mother with reminisces of days gone by. Perhaps that created a distrust in cherished objects and shocked her with the reality of the phantom nature of money. But Boston was still home. She reveled in the clang of passing trolleys, the grind of subway wheels, and the chime of the Chicago World's Fair clock. This cacophony of nostalgic sounds revived her enchanted past and rekindled her passion for dreams not yet realized.

The lady behind the Continental podium announced boarding would begin.

"Let's go at last call," I suggested

Daddyo got up. "Jesus," he said, "you'd be late for your own funeral. Now where the hell's your mother?"

We joined the line forming at the tunnel's mouth. Troy ambled over and stood beside us.

My mother and Jen hustled out of the gift shop with leis. They took turns dropping leis over my head and kissing my cheek. We hugged. I promised to write once a week.

Troy held out his hand. "Rotsa ruck, Kirbo."

We shook. I felt the callouses on his hand and felt bad our brotherhood was in shambles. He existed in a land of pain and resentment that made getting close impossible. Being alone with our father made him hate me more.

"Time to go," Daddyo said.

We entered the tunnel. Going to college was exciting but I felt I bad for my kid sister. The voices continued. The yelling of new nuns had replaced those of the old. The only thing that buoyed her spirits was clinging to the dream of becoming a rock star.

My father found our seats in the middle aisle near the back of the plane, opposite the emergency door window.

"Remove those leis," my father said.

"Why?"

He waved a limp wrist. "People in Denver will think you're one of those."

Daddyo had reserved us a room at The Brown Palace, the only hotel he knew in Colorado. He'd stayed there in 1949 during his red convertible journey from Boston and dined on Rocky Mountain Oysters in the restaurant. He wondered if ram balls were still in fashion.

"Full of iron," Daddyo had told me.

"How'd they taste?"

"Like Swedish meatballs, but more gamy."

We taxied over the tarmac between rows of green lights. The jet engines roared, powering us down the runway and up. I spotted the blue rings of La Ronde through the emergency window and the red lights at the Top of the Waikiki. I thought about Laura. She'd left early for summer school at Lewis & Clark and her parents didn't seem pleased when I showed up at her gate. We'd only dated twice. She hadn't planned to visit Colorado and I wasn't heading to Oregon anytime soon.

My father craned his neck gazing over the seat in front of him. He signaled a blonde stewardess. She strutted over, a gold dress hugging her hourglass figure. "Yes, Sir?" she asked. The hem of her dress was cut mid-thigh and a gold jet pin glistened above her breast.

"May I order a gin martini, Miss?" my father asked.

"Absolutely, Sir. With or without an olive?"

"With."

"Would your boy care for a refreshment?"

"No, thanks," I said.

She winked at my father. "Back in a jiffy."

My father watched her head for the galley. He elbowed me. "Cheesus," he muttered, "if I were single, I'd really go that."

The stewardess returned with the martini. My father unlocked his tray table and she placed a napkin and his drink in the slot.

"Thank you, Miss," my father said, handing her a ten. "Keep the change."

She smiled. "Holler for Linda if you gents need anything at all."

"I certainly will," he said and watched her saunter off. He stuck an index finger in the drink, stirred slowly, and the olive spun. He sipped and smacked his lips, as if tasting something bitter. "When do classes start, Kirby?" he asked.

"Monday," I replied.

"What's your first subject?"

"Writing."

"Good. Your professor will make you analyze texts and compose essays. Didn't you write essays at Punahou?"

"Yes."

"What were your grades?"

"I don't remember."

"You don't remember because your grades were poor."

Daddyo said my mediocre GPA was proof of my laziness and the CU admissions committee only gave me the green light because they wanted my out-of-state tuition. He was so driven hunting down flaws that he failed to see anything good. I wasn't his solo target. He considered my mother a birdbrain and a spendthrift. He thought Troy shared my mother's low IQ and would do little with his life. He believed Jen's lack of willpower branded her a loser. Hatred was his fuel. He used us as pumps to propel his glorious engine forward, a rage machine forged during his impoverished Kaimuki childhood. I could tell he'd invested in me flopping in academia. But he was oblivious that I'd been studying him. His speech, gestures, and mannerisms revealed someone who took delight in ripping others apart. His soul fed off his never-ending resentment. Daddyo had never praised Troy or me for anything in high school. In his mind, he'd given us advantages he never had but we foolishly squandered his gifts. His contempt was rooted in his hanai upbringing and abuse from his uncles. They'd found his secret place and stole his savings, invited him to pretend dinners at Wo Fats, and tormented him for being a bastard. Uncle Sharkey had thrown him off the dock at Fisherman's Wharf and called down, "Sink o' swim, punk." I grieved for him. But I also realized that, instead of learning from his past, he was punishing our family for his years of suffering.

My thoughts drifted to Troy. He worked a pick-and-shovel job but loved manual labor. He'd said flies swarmed his plate lunches and scorpions crawled the interior walls of the Porto-Potty in Waikiki. Our final summer on Moloka'i had been bittersweet. Troy had been more communicative in the primal setting of Wailau but I realized we were heading in opposite directions

I pulled Jen's envelope from my back pocket and opened it. It was a Bon Voyage card. She wished me a safe flight and added a special take on an Elton John classic:

Kirby my brother you are older than me
Do you still feel the pain of the scars that won't heal
Your eyes have died but you see more than I
Kirby, you're a star in the face of the sky
Oh God it looks like Kirby, must be the clouds in my eyes

I tucked the card back in the envelope and folded it to fit my front pocket. I'd pretended those scars no longer hurt and that our father hadn't killed her innocence. But I knew Creature World and my attempts to save my sister had fallen short. She would return to her pink room knowing I was no longer behind the wall we shared. I prayed that someday in her adult life Jen would find someone to love her big, enough to make up for years of suffering.

THE pilot said the sun was breaking over the Rockies. I sprung up and looked out the emergency door window. The land below resembled crumpled brown wrap. We flew above jagged ridges and bone-dry plains. Everything felt like a mistake—traveling with my father, heading east to school, and attending a university overrun with strangers. I returned to my seat. Daddyo stretched. He gulped orange juice. His hair was more salt than pepper. His sideburns looked raggedy. He folded his tray, locked it in place, and rattled a cup of ice.

I examined my leis: the plumeria had turned brown and the orchids hung limp. I yanked the garlands off and jammed them into the seat pocket holding magazines.

A chubby steward headed down the aisle. He had red hair and looked grumpy.

"Say, fellow," Daddyo waved, "what's Denver's current temperature?"

"Fifty-two," the steward answered. "But it'll warm to seventy-five."

"They call it 'The Mile High City,' don't they?"

"That's right, sir."

My father handed the steward his cup. "Just think," he said, "a village in the clouds."

We rented a Buick Skylark and rambled to Denver. We ordered omelets at a greasy spoon on Colfax before checking into the Brown Palace. The crimson carpet in our room was threadbare. The room reeked of cigar smoke. There were twin beds side-by-side, a TV with rabbit-ears, and silver ashtrays made of plastic. I flopped on a bed. The springs creaked.

My father stripped to his underwear and sat on the edge of his bed. He plucked the phone's receiver out of its cradle. "I need a wake-up call tomorrow morning," he said. "Six sharp."

I shut my eyes. I dreamt I was on a lounge chair at the Diamond Head Beach Hotel. The clouds clung battleship gray to the horizon. I peeled my legs from the straps and stood on a lawn edged with naupaka. A sail cut a jagged path through the whitecaps. A wrinkled man emerged from the coconut shadows and spread his towel over a yellow square of light. His back was as red as a boiled crab. I heard gears churning, rolling. A conveyor belt carried bodies into the flames of a shoreline crematorium. Pipes spewed ashes into the sea. The shallows clouded. A tide moved in and carried the ashes beyond the breakers.

Someone shook my shoulder. "Get ready for dinner, Kirby."

19TH Century European warfare was the theme of The Palace Arms Restaurant. Military regalia decorated the maroon walls, including skinny rifles with bayonets and swords from the Napoleonic Wars. There were candelabras, crystal chandeliers, and gold flags with fleur-de-lys emblems. Waiters rushed by in purple tuxedos. My old man was disappointed Rocky Mountain Oysters weren't on the menu. He ordered a double martini from a French maid waitress. A Hispanic waiter took our order.

"Kirby," my father said, "have you picked a major yet?"

I tasted my water. "English."

"Very good. Writing papers teaches you to think critically."

"I like a different kind of writing."

"Oh? And what kind is that?"

"Poetry."

His eyes bulged out. "Poetry doesn't pay a goddamn thing," he said, "you know that."

"Some poets make money."

"Name one."

"Robert Frost."

"Only because JFK had him recite at his inauguration. Ninety-nine percent of poets don't have a pot to pee in."

"Allen Ginsberg has a pot."

"Ginsberg's a Columbia drop-out and a mahu. You'd better not follow in his footsteps."

"But he's rich and famous."

"Look, Kirby, you didn't come all the way to Colorado to write poetry. You'll end up digging ditches alongside your brother."

"Troy works construction."

Daddyo pulled off his glasses. "Construction in Waikiki means manual labor. Guess what's under all that asphalt."

"Coral?"

"Water, and lots of it. I should know, I draw up all the big contracts."

"Troy makes decent money."

"It may seem decent now," Daddyo said, "but it won't support a family. Your brother's in for a rude awakening."

"What if he starts his own company?"

"I'll give Troy one year to come to his senses. If he doesn't attend college, he's getting booted out on his okole." The waiter delivered trout on white platters shaped like fish. The dinners included rice pilaf, steamed broccoli, and a sprig of mint. "Careful, gentlemen," the waiter warned, "these plates are mighty hot."

"That looks good,'" Daddyo said. "Doesn't it look good, son?"

"Yes."

"May I fetch you gentlemen some tartar sauce?"

Daddyo held up his hand. "None for me."

"Count me in," I said.

The waiter nodded and left.

My father cleared his throat. "Now, Kirby, there's something I've been meaning to tell you, something I've been noticing."

I squeezed lemon over my trout and took a bite. The fish was bland compared to mahi-mahi. "What have you noticed?" I asked.

"You're constantly pulling this wise guy routine, like a jerk with a chip on his shoulder. That might land you in trouble at the university."

"I'll avoid trouble."

"Nobody likes a wise guy. Some big football player might get mad and clobber you."

"I'll be fine."

"Okay, but don't come crawling to me if you get in a scrape."

"I won't," I promised, "even if I end up in jail."

DADDYO snored in our room. I headed for the window and looked down at the traffic on 17th Street. The air smelled of burnt oil. I thought about my father's childhood days when he slept on a cot in the parlor. Bobby and Granny slept on cots too. Granny's sons had the bedrooms. Dad Hickman, the gentleman boarder, slept outside under the eave. My father remembered Uncle Carlos, the lawyer brother who'd stolen his grandmother's land. He'd been determined to make good in school so nobody could do to him what Carlos had done to Granny. He'd watched her roll off her cot, open the screen door, and slip under Hickman's mosquito netting.

WE sped for Boulder after a continental breakfast. I'd found brochures in the lobby and fingered them riding shotgun. A brochure sprung open like an accordion. "Let's see the sights," I said.

"What sights?" Daddyo asked.

"Pike's Peak and Aspen. There's this big brewery in Golden."

"That's a waste of time."

"Isn't Coors beer your favorite?"

"Yes."

"You can drink all you want for free."

Daddyo sneezed. The windshield smelled like old sneakers. "Look," he said, "I won't drive willy nilly all over Kingdom sightseeing. You're damn lucky you're not alone on a bus instead of being escorted to Boulder like a prince."

We headed through fields of wheat stretching east. A threshing machine resembled a praying mantis. We passed a house with a barn, hay stacks, and cows behind fences. The cow eyes looked sad. There was a big tank on stilts with GAS painted bright red on its side.

"I have responsibilities," Daddyo explained. "You'll learn more about that after you're married."

He sneezed again. Droplets speckled the windshield. He pulled a handkerchief and blew. It was as if all the joy and wonder had been squeezed out of him, reducing him to the pulpless rind of a man. He'd never believed you could see the moon in the afternoon and, when I pointed it out, he refused to look up. He followed his own set of rules and challenging him was a no-win situation. I switched on the radio, spun the dial, and settled on "Everybody is a Star."

My father winced. "You like that crap?"

"Thought you liked Diana Ross?"

"That's not her. Turn it to the news."

WE hoofed it around campus, opened a checking account, and lunched on burgers at the Alfred E. Packer Grill. Troy was right. My father's expectations made me feel as though my life wasn't my own. We found the Boulder Mall and entered Montgomery Wards. The AC blew hard.

A salesman with a brown tie greeted us. "May I be of some service today?"

"I need threads," I said.

"What do the college students wear?" Daddyo asked.

"Follow me," the salesman replied and led us to Men's Clothing.

I pulled on an orange down jacket. It fit snug and felt warm.

"Too loud," my father said. He dug through the sales rack and found a dirt-brown jacket with a thin lining. "Now this is more like it," he said. He picked out boots, two pairs of jeans, and three flannel shirts

"Need BVDs?" he asked.

"Got plenty."

"Good. Let's find your dorm and get dinner. I've gotta long drive back to Denver."

Baker Hall was in the center of campus. I'd been accepted late and it was the only dorm with rooms still available. The building was deserted.

"What beautiful red brick," Daddyo said, "just beautiful."

We found the Headmaster's office on the first floor. A black secretary handed my father the key to my room. She warned us there was no heat.

"My boy can take it," Daddyo said.

She handed me a wool blanket. "The nights do get cold."

My room was in the basement. The names of my two roommates—*Gary Rennecker and Michael Dyes*—were typed on a yellow index card taped to the door. I slid in the key and turned the knob. The door didn't budge. I slammed my shoulder against the wood paneling—the door sprung open.

My father located the light switch on the wall. A bare bulb on the ceiling lit up a room with beige walls, a single bed, and a set of bunk beds. There was the aroma of disinfectant. Two desks were against the far wall.

I tossed my blanket on the single bed, swung up my suitcase, and unzipped it.

Daddyo watched me stuff shirts, pants, and underwear into a chest of drawers. "This is a good room for studying," he told me.

Before leaving, my father knocked on the Resident Advisor's door down the hall. A tall guy wearing a white Izod shirt appeared. He introduced himself as JD Culhane and said he pitched for the Buffaloes.

"Buffaloes?" I asked.

"The school mascot," JD replied.

"What's your major, JD?" Daddyo asked.

"English."

"Plan to become a teacher?"

"I'm applying to law school."

"Kirby, did you hear that? JD's going to law school."

JD looked at me and shrugged his shoulders.

"That's an admirable goal," my father said. "Your parents must be proud."

"Doc Culhane would prefer I pursue medicine. He's head surgeon at the Mayo Clinic."

"I went to Harvard myself, JD. Take it from me, law school is the place to go, even if you don't wanna practice."

"You graduated Harvard?"

"Thanks to good grades and the GI Bill. It was far from a cakewalk but I gutted it out."

"I'll keep an eye on your boy."

"I'd appreciate it," Daddyo said. "He's very green."

"How old are you anyway?" JD asked me.

"Seventeen."

OUR last meal was at the Chophouse & Tavern. We took a booth and ordered T-bones from a brunette with a "Mandy" nametag. The bridge of her nose was saddled with freckles and she wore a blue-and-white striped blouse over white bellbottoms. She brought out plates with sizzling steaks.

"Vino?" Mandy asked.

Daddyo studied the Wine List. "You a skier, Mandy?"

"Does it show?"

"You seem athletic," my father replied. "I'll have a bottle of the Chablis."

"With pleasure," Mandy said and skipped away.

"Gee," Daddyo muttered, "that Mandy's a good looker'. If I were back in college, I'd really go for her." He took off his glasses and stuck them beside the wine glass. "Look," he said, "this is your golden opportunity to meet lotsa girls."

I cut around the bone in my steak. "What about Laura?"

"Where'd she go?"

"Lewis & Clark, in Portland."

"Mainland guys really go for Orientals. They find 'em exotic."

I stabbed a piece of meat. "I might transfer."

"Transfer, nothing." He cut his steak and forked a piece in his mouth. "With mainland girls," he advised while chewing, "no shy stuff. If you like a girl, tell her right off the bat you're from Hawaii. That'll set you apart."

"I'll say I'm part Hawaiian."

He rested his utensils on his plate. "I'm not sure what your grandmother told you, but you have very little Hawaiian blood."

"Your eighth makes me a sixteenth."

"Nobody knows the exact amount. I wouldn't advertise it."

"I'm proud to be local."

"You should be more proud you're mostly English and Irish."

Mandy plopped an ice bucket on our table, removed the bottle's foil seal, and popped the cork. My father sniffed the cork as wine gurgled into the glass.

He sipped. "Nice bouquet."

Mandy sunk the bottle into the ice. "I think so too." She left us to wait on a table of bearded men wearing jackets with elbow patches.

My father smacked his lips. "Don't forget Hawaii. That excites 'em."

"Did it excite Mom?"

"Geography was never her strong suit. Why, your mother didn't even know where Hawaii was. She liked me because I was a good dancer and treated her to lobster dinners and shows. Another thing to remember is never get serious about a first girl. That'll be Troy. Bet he ends up marrying the first wahine who looks his way. That guy never thinks."

"Like a chicken with its head cut off," I said.

"That's right. Not thinking, not using his brain. Most men who marry that first girl get divorced, like your mother's father. Play the field, that's my advice."

"Did you play the field?"

"Oh, boy," he chuckled. "Boy, did I."

After we finished, Mandy stacked our plates. "Dessert tonight?" she asked.

"None for me," Daddyo said, patting his belly. "How 'bout you, Kirbo?"

"I'll pass."

Mandy split for the kitchen. But she soon reappeared, balancing a tray of mugs and two pitchers of beer. She put the tray down on a table with upperclassmen. Mandy filled their mugs. A guy with a white turtleneck rambled on about how our football team could never beat Nebraska and, when the Cornhuskers beat us again, he'd streak the Lincoln sidelines.

Daddyo peeled the label off the bottle. "Dating helps you decide what it is you want in a girl," he said. "I dated quite a bit in Boston before meeting your mother."

"She go out much?"

"She liked this effeminate grad at MIT who made her type his thesis. Then along comes this Fletcher character who sells his blood to pay for dinner at the wharf. Can you guess what he did during the date?"

"What?"

"Nibbled breadsticks while your mother ate her lobster. He told her he had a stomach ache but I bet he couldn't afford two meals."

"Now he's a millionaire."

"Who's a millionaire?"

"Fletcher."

"Come on."

"He invented polyester. Mom said so."

Daddyo rolled the label into a ball. "That's what he tells fools in Boston, like your mother's brother. But I'm sure he played a very small part in its invention. Fletcher's one of these scientists who makes twenty thousand a year bent all day over a Bunsen burner."

"Twenty thousand? That's it?"

"If he's lucky."

"Wow. So why'd you choose Mom?"

"June was a wholesome girl." He leaned over and whispered, "she was a virgin." He stuffed the balled-up label into the bottle's mouth. "You don't want a girl who's been with lotsa men." He gazed out the window. Coeds in tight jeans and Kappa Delta sweatshirts giggled by. "Cheesus," he said, "everywhere I look, beautiful girls. Invite them to good restaurants. They won't forget you if you take them to nice places."

I wasn't sure how I could afford dinner dates with ninety bucks at Boulder Savings.

Mandy brought our bill. "Sure I can't tempt you?" she asked my father. "We have scrumptious apple pie."

"I'm too full, Mandy. Say, when's the first snow?"

"Usually near Halloween." She waved over at the white turtleneck guy.

150

His buddies were slamming quarters against the table trying to bounce them into their mugs.

The turtleneck guy winked. "I'm in lust."

Mandy giggled and headed over. He scooted out his chair out and she sat on his lap. She stroked his hair. He nibbled her ear.

"Exercise vigorously," Daddyo advised. "That'll help with studies. No exercise makes you fat and lethargic."

"I'll shadowbox and jog."

"Careful of personal hygiene. Girls don't like stinky men."

"I don't stink."

"Not sure if you noticed, but your brother has horrible halitosis and horrendous BO."

Whenever my father was alone with Troy, he'd rake me over the coals. My brother had always been eager to share Daddyo's laundry list of complaints against me.

"Even stinkers get dates," I said. "Troy's problem is no confidence. Things might have been different if you'd praised him once in a while."

My father's cheeks flared red. "Kirby, you're one of these kids who blames his parents for everything and anything that goes wrong. That's a good way to shirk responsibility."

"We're talking about Troy, not me."

"Funny, I had no mother and no father. Look how well I turned out."

"You did?"

"Don't get smart, wise guy. I had nothing compared to you boys but I pulled myself up by my bootstraps."

"You weren't an easy father."

"At least you had one."

Daddyo paid. We wandered The Hill district, passing clothing stores, art galleries, and a dojo. The moon lit up the oaks lining Broadway. I spotted the Skylark. My father unlocked the driver's door. A truck groaned up the incline.

My father checked his Timex. "Cheesus," he said, "late, late, late. Can you find your way back to Baker Hall?"

"Yes."

He held out his hand. "Well, good-bye and good luck."

We shook like strangers. I didn't want to end it that way. I didn't want my father leaving without saying something heartfelt, something I could carry around inside of me. "Daddy, what are you made of?"

"What?"

"What are you made of?"

"I guess I'm made of iron. That's it. Iron. What are you made of, son?"

"Steel," I replied. "I've always been made of steel." I grabbed his shoulder. He let me hug him before dropping down into the driver's seat.

He powered down his window. "Lose the wise guy stuff. Promise?"

"Promise."

"Good boy."

I stood at the curb while he pulled away. The Skylark tooled down Broadway. Jazz came from Tulagi's Pizza. His car hung a left off Broadway and vanished behind a Texaco station.

I eased between oaks and jogged crossing Broadway. This was my chance to create a new me. I decided to wipe the slate clean skirting the amphitheater. I crossed paths with a pack of coeds heading for The Hill.

"Howzit," I said.

A redhead smiled. "Go Buffs."

I reached Baker Hall and took the stairway down to the basement. Boxes were stacked outside the neighboring room. I unlocked the door, shouldered it open, and locked it behind me. I switched on the light. I tested the bunk bed mattresses and considered the top bunk. Instead, I spread my blanket over the single bed and flicked the light off. The moon lit up the door. Laura entered my thoughts. I had this crazy urge to hop a Greyhound bound for Portland. I heard footsteps in the hall. A hinge creaked. I'd come a long way to find someplace lonely but knew that feeling would pass. I imagined my father on the flight home. He'd flirt with the stewardess and order martinis. He'd jiggle change in his pocket and stretch. He'd check and re-check his Timex.

The man of iron was gone. Part of me was relieved. But a bigger part hungered for his approval. I wanted to give him some reason to love me. After all, I was his son.

I saw us driving the twilight fields south of Boulder. The radio played "Rocky Mountain High." I invented a father who was there to pick me up whenever I faltered, a man who gave me credit for trying and never shamed me for coming up short. He pointed at the Denver lights and drummed his palms on the wheel to the beat of the song. He said my future was near those lights, somewhere in the sea of shadows beyond the city.

WHYTE BEACH

Most locals don't know it exists, it's not named on any maps and the approach is difficult, almost impossible at high tide along the shoreline. We scrambled over slippery rocks, avoided a hornet's nest and seaweed shaped like a noose, one misplaced foot might sweep you into the ocean. From the beach we could see multiple islands and there was actual sand, not just pebbles. Worth the trip, my friend said, crouching beside a blanched starfish in the tidal pool. Yeah, I said, but if anyone asks we're supposed to say we parked by the main beach and walked along the shoreline, which is what we did. Why would anyone ask? he asked. We approached the right way so it doesn't matter. Why would anyone care how we got here? I heard the people here don't like it if you use the path by the road, I said, gesturing behind us at the beachfront homes. But this is a public beach, he said. Yeah but the people here wouldn't like it if they knew we used the path, which we didn't, that's what someone told me so if anyone asks. No one should ask, my friend said. We stared at pale clouds forming along the horizon before clambering back over the rocks. The tide was coming in.

TRANSFORMATIONS

Foxes ghosted, but what was the point
for our cat without the wideness of life?
So out she went,
until bitten and paralysis slowly set in.
At first it was just a stuttered walk,
which we hoped would pass.
She managed the steps for a while,
but they grew in time.
Later, when she couldn't move at all,
she came to us through sound,
insistently, like when she was young
and a closed door
separated her from food.
She looked at me in a way
that asked if I could be a bridge
to what she was before,
that I was her great hope.
But what could anyone do?
My father's gaze in comparison is vacant,
perhaps realizing that memory
is the best way back,
or just that he has seen enough.
It is partly the Parkinson's I guess.
We used to play catch in our garden.
He gave me my first baseball glove,
helped me to break it in.
Now he might not walk, or call

out to the past with talk,
but I can still feel
the momentum of that day,
throwing back and forth,
as he taught torque, rhythm,

and how it all fit together.

A KADDISH FOR CASPAR GLASS

CASPAR Glass, trusts and estates, worked alone in his corner office, high above the darkening city. His last client of the day, Harry Oxman, 76, the seventh generation of Oxman in the United States, left after directing that Glass rewrite Oxman's will to bequeath a $5 million lump sum payment to his current paramour upon his death, provided she remained his paramour at the time of his passing. Glass asked Oxman, his client of thirty years, "And how, Harry, shall we establish that she remained your paramour up until your death? Will you be providing regular updates?" Oxman appeared to consider it and then rasped, "Caspar, just make it happen like you always do," laboring out of the chair while waving off Glass's help; which Glass had not offered. Oxman shuffled toward the closed door of Glass' office. Without turning around, he growled into his shoulder, "Need I say this must be secret Caspar? The rest of the family, especially Emily, can't know." No, you needn't, Glass thought.

Oxman opened the office door, and Glass saw his paramour, Brie, a young woman of 26, knees together bent like a skier, practically vibrating with anticipation. She pecked Oxman on the cheek and wrapped him with a lithe arm, steadying him for the walk to the elevator. Glass consoled himself tartly that the proof that she remained Oxman's paramour at his death would be manifest as Oxman seemed a sure bet to die with Brie *in flagrante delicto* (likely Harry's heart failing), *res ipsa loquitur* (Brie birthday-suited on scene calling Glass from bedside for help and as proof), *requiescat in pace* (Harry in the ground and Brie in the money). And then, as the children's rhyme goes, the cheese would stand alone.

Later, Oxman's family would ask Glass about Harry's deception, his faithlessness, and what other Harry Oxman secrets Glass knew, and why oh why would Harry do it. This would all lead to the question of whether

Brie could be cut out of the will. This was how it often went.

For decades, Glass had created secret trusts, rewritten wills, and drafted codicils deciding the fates and fortunes, and even emotional well-being, of his clients' family members, the unwitting characters in each client's drama. Of course, he tried to counsel his clients not to indulge their baser feelings and make a spouse feel diminished, or a child rejected, or more positively to honor the emotional attachments of family members, if not for them then – and here he played on a client's vanity – so that the client would be viewed as a great patriarch or matriarch and regarded well privately and publicly. He had always executed his client's testamentary directions with discretion and perfect equanimity, no matter how injurious to the family Glass knew they would be. Like any good trusts and estates lawyer he could keep secrets.

But over the last year, Glass had begun to lose his calm and become — unprofessionally in his view — disturbed by his connection to the pain his clients often sprung on their families. What made Glass anxious was the knowledge that many of his clients had enmeshed their families in the client's lies only for the family to discover the falsity of their lives after the client's death — too late to do anything about it.

Not just Oxman. In nearly every family he dealt with, the secrets lay buried like unexploded mines. Glass knew these minefields inside out. Clients retained him to map them, re-map them, and then clean up after the explosion. What gnawed at him was why, after all he had been through and after all these years, other people's secrets should cause him anxiety, or some other vague diagnosis of nervous disorder, as Lansman had suggested. It was when he started to feel on the verge of unraveling, although it was invisible to others, that he went to see Lansman, a client who was a shrink. Lansman, with pink skin hung like bunting below his watery eyes as if every patient weighed on him, suggested they meet for sessions to get to the bottom of why Glass "could no longer compartmentalize his work." This was how Glass had put it, and Lansman quoted it back. "Caspar these symptoms are more than that and mainly come from trauma." Glass said, "mainly" he just wanted a valium prescription. Lansman gave him the prescription, on the promise that Glass would see him soon. Glass didn't. Even when the symptoms grew more difficult to control, he felt he could manage them without discussing his past with Lansman, or any doctor.

So once again, alone in his office, feeling the unraveling coming on, Glass reviewed his own case. He thought back forty years to a frozen forest in Europe. He and others waited in silence, half-buried in the ground under pine spires clotted with snow. Nothing moved except plumes of breath. The cold, a blade on your skin. Then the whistles and screams of bombs and everything blasted open in fiery chaos with shock waves that knocked him flat whipping him with sheets of dirt and snow. Trees splintered open, black charred craters burst like abscesses in the snow, and limbs flung themselves from bodies. In between explosions, the agonized calls of soldiers came from nowhere and everywhere at once. Men died alone, eventually frozen stiff. But he survived.

He survived, too, snipers and close combat in burned-out cities. Cities where civilization proved to be a pretty façade of cathedrals and cafés. Until the façade was tested by a few madmen and collapsed. Speeches, parades, bonfires, broken glass, and eventually so many ready to play along. 'Civilization' that with the slightest push — the slightest excuse really — could incinerate and bury itself in bodies and rubble. The white baby shoe that stood upright on a cobble-stoned street in front of a door with nothing but rubble behind it. They tore off the mask of decency and then, defeated, some ashamed, some just exhausted, put it back on again until the next time.

In 1945 he came home, stunned and alone. With no idea what to do, he became a lawyer because law felt like a distracting puzzle. He kept unwanted memories tamped down. He learned to shut them off from causing any feeling at all. That experience now belonged to someone else. What a relief, but what an absurdity it was too, to have a job or a profession after you have been among men killing, dying and screaming for the medic or their mother. And what a sad joke on him, after the horrors he saw decades ago, that in New York in 1983 the secrets and lies of his clients should make him anxious, or even affect his mind one whit. He kneaded a cramp in his chest. Something from lunch didn't agree with him.

Miriam wasn't at her desk. She hadn't said goodbye, so Glass assumed she was filing or in the bathroom. Through the bank of windows he saw the river. The October sky lowered an ashen light. In other buildings, office lights flicked off as people left for the night. He thought he should go home. He turned on his desk lamp and made brief notes in Oxman's file.

He sat back in his chair. His office, lustrous with wood and leather, was dead quiet. Old prints of sailing ships and a map of New York harbor and lower Manhattan, as it was in the 18th century, lined the far wall. The door to his burled barrister's armoire, a gift from British lawyers for whom he had lectured on U.S. intestacy law, was open. His hat sat on the top shelf. His spare suit hung with his spare shoes directly below, like an invisible man. He could see himself in the mirror on the inside of the door, underlit by the green desk light. He looked indistinct. He couldn't understand why the door to the armoire was open, but instead of getting up to close it, he sat in silence.

It had been a long time since he last looked at it. He unlocked the bottom drawer of his desk and took out the small box. He lifted the leather cuff of the desk blotter and felt with one finger for the key, which he kept taped down between the leather and the blotting paper. He unlocked the box. The worn metal dog tag had no chain anymore. He ran his finger over his name debossed in black letters in the metal: CHARLES F. GREEN; his serial number; T43 for his tetanus shot in 1943; and O, his blood type. The bottom right corner of the tag was cut and sharp, and still showed where it was burned.

It was at night near the Belgian-German border, sitting with Strauss, Stone, and Rosenthal, that he cut the H from his tag. After that, he held his Zippo under the cut edge, and the flame wrapped like a blue tongue around the metal until it turned black. He burned it to make it look like it happened in battle. He threw his other tag into the woods because two of them mutilated in the same place would never be believed. But he couldn't bring himself to throw both tags away and have no identity if he were killed. Forty years and he could still hear the snap of the metal being cut and then the smell of it burning. Renunciation. Disguise. Fear.

Because word had gone around that if you were captured with an "H" on your tag there was no chance you would live.

Rosenthal, pale as chalk and skinny with a jutting Adam's apple, said it wasn't right, it wasn't permitted under Jewish law.

'Put a lid on it Rebbe,' said Strauss. A week earlier, Strauss found a kid who used to engrave at a jeweler's on Canal Street. Strauss gave him a tube of M&Ms in exchange for him changing Strauss' "H" to a "P". 'Rosy, you don't get to make a ruling cause with your name, the "H" is super-, super- . . . goddamnit . . . Greenie at least has a fighting chance to pass.'

Stone, who the day before had put his tag on a tree stump and used his Colt to shoot out the "H" and about a third of the tag, was cleaning his gun. He didn't look up or stop when he said 'for the Protestants it's a "P" and the Catholics a "C", but for Jews it's not "J", it's "H" for Hebrew, like we're foreigners, like a different race.'

Strauss said, 'Who does that remind you of? Why not just say on the tag "hey Kraut, if captured, you'll definitely want to kill this guy."'

Rosenthal shrugged, 'It's not allowed to deny you're a Jew.'

Stone closed one eye to look in the chamber of his pistol, 'Who's denying? He's just not admitting.'

Strauss barked 'yeah, Green looks like some Ivy league tennis player but Rosy, you practically scream Jew. Anyway *tzaddik*, where is it written you can't do it?'

Stone said, 'It's definitely not one of the Ten Commandments. That's as far as I can go. Rosy, ya gotta cite a law or something.'

It ended there with Rosenthal shaking his head and walking away into the dark, his last words, 'It's wrong. And Strauss, the word is superfluous . . . moron.' He left everyone laughing, calling for him to come back.

Glass squeezed the cramp in his chest, and it felt better for a moment. He thought he heard noise in the hall but still didn't see Miriam at her desk.

WITHOUT a knock or a word, in strode Fenster: portly but cat-footed, a beard like smoke, black suit, white rumpled button-down bloused at the belt-line, black dented Homburg. He sat himself down facing Glass like he owned the place. Glass, surprised, but wanting to exude calm, leaned back in his chair and looked him over.

"You are?"

"Solomon Fenster." The man's voice was gravel.

"I don't believe I've had the pleasure."

"Oh, ho, the pleasure? Let's wait and see."

"I'm sorry – did you make an appointment with my secretary because I don't think you're scheduled."

"I don't know from your schedule but I have an appointment. I'm here for our talk. For counsel. You don't recognize me?" Fenster tipped up the front brim of his hat, widened his eyes and craned forward for Glass to inspect his face.

Glass studied him. He seemed familiar somehow, but Glass was in no mood. "No."

"You know me. Stanton Street?"

Glass felt the threat in Fenster like some buried evidence about to yield itself up from the ground. "No, you're mistaken."

"Yes, yes, think."

"You should leave Mr. Fenster, it's late. Make an appointment."

"I have an appointment. And it's for now."

Glass looked, but Miriam was still not at her desk.

"Listen Glass, or should I call you Green? Makes no difference to me what you call yourself and what you pretend to be." Fenster swiveled his head to scan the walls. "You've done well for yourself these years. Tell me, Glass, what fine things you see from your chair? Or what magnificent view out the window? Because I don't see it."

Glass stared straight at Fenster. "What do you want?"

"I need help. I've done well too, Glass. I'm a doctor with assets here and there. But my oldest daughter has strayed. She's a smart and beautiful girl, but she's headstrong. Anyway the story of her life you don't need to know except this. She's with a Gentile, against my wishes, and I think she'll marry him if he asks. This cannot be allowed to happen."

"Why not?"

"Why not? It's completely out of the question. He wants her to convert."

Glass didn't respond. Fenster seemed completely unbothered by the silence, drumming his pen on a small notebook, giving Glass and his desk the once-over. Where in God's name was Miriam?

Finally, Glass spoke. "What's this have to do with me anyway, Mr. uh —?"

"Fenster. You don't listen so great for a lawyer." He went to close the office door and returned to the chair. "This is private stuff. It's got everything to do with you. I want her cut off from any of my assets if she marries out of the faith. I want that in my will. I want you to do that. The law permits that, right Glass?"

Glass nodded. "The law permits it."

"And I want some sort of whattayacallit agreement before she marries him that says he doesn't get any of her money, my money, if she turns her back."

"A pre-nuptial agreement."

"Right – one of those."

"You should talk with your daughter. She'll end up hating you. Talk with your rabbi. This is not the shtetl after all. This is 1983."

"Not the shtetl! 1983! Listen to you Glass. Anyway, you don't think I've tried talking to my daughter?"

"But why come to me? You could get this done somewhere else. I'm not the lawyer for you."

"Wrong. This is sensitive. I don't want anyone with connections to the community involved. I want it quiet. You do some legal thing that stops this, or tell me why I shouldn't." Fenster's tone changed suddenly almost pleading to Glass, "Green, Glass, I don't care. I'll keep your secret. But I came to you because you know what it means to cut yourself off, to leave your family and your history. I need someone to tell me why, why would she do that? I want to stop her but maybe I shouldn't. What will happen to her if she cuts herself off from her family and her history?"

"How would I know? She's your daughter. Maybe she's in love. Maybe she just wants distance. Frankly, Fenster, you don't seem like a day at the beach as a father."

"You do know because you did the same."

Glass, against his instincts, answered. "Mine wasn't at all the same.

Yes, for sure love, but circumstances were different."

"Ah, circumstances, you lawyers and your circumstances, but at least we are back on track Glass even if you claim we haven't spoken before. Please continue." Fenster moved forward in the chair and began leafing through his notebook. Strangely, Glass began to feel drawn to Fenster, not that he liked this man, but that he had the urge to talk to him as if they had unfinished business.

"Okay, I'll play along. I'll start with the war, just facts and history. I'm not interested in spiritual counseling. Draw your own conclusions." Fenster came to a blank page and looked at Glass with his pen poised.

"The soldiers were mostly good men, and mostly the same. Same uniforms, same haircuts, same enemy, same fear. There were Jews. We'd find each other. Sometimes it was made clear to us we weren't welcome, but for the most part we were accepted because, after all, we could save a fellow soldier's life or die as well as the next man.

"Stone, Strauss and I all made it out of the war alive. Rosenthal disappeared after the Hürtgen Forest. Like in a fairy tale, he just vanished in dark German woods. If he had been dead, it would have been better. But no, later we learned German wolves had gotten him, truly wolves, with blood all over their snouts, and their faces twisted with rabid fury, always hunting and killing. We thought Rosenthal was dead, but he was alive and we didn't know. He had the bad luck to be taken prisoner. They tortured them, worked them to the bone, and starved them, and then, later, when the Russians and the Americans were closing in, the wolves, insane until the end, forced the prisoners out on a death march. Men weighing under 100 pounds, sick and delirious, collapsed along the road and died. They made the surviving prisoners bury the bodies along the way to hide the evidence. Roosevelt was already dead. Hitler in days would be dead in his bunker, and the Germans would surrender. But Rosy, it turns out, was still alive, marching."

Glass stopped, choking on his thoughts, now regretting going through this again.

Fenster said flatly. "Go on, Glass. This is not the end."

"But this has nothing to do with your matter."

"Go on."

"They wouldn't stop. It was April 1945. They marched these wasted men south on a road along a black river, swollen with snow-melt, past picturesque towns and gingerbread houses. The people gawked at the walking skeletons. Some were moved to offer food, some just spat at the sight of them and cursed them. The prisoners died everyday along the road. We learned Rosenthal tried to escape into the forest only to be caught and beaten. Why? What did it matter? Everyone knew the war was over. If they had just let him go, he likely would have died in the forest peacefully like a leaf that just finally lets go from a tree."

Fenster frowned at this and seemed to cross something out. He propped his elbow on the arm of the chair and rested his cheek on the palm of his fleshy hand. He exhaled wearily.

"I am boring you perhaps?" Glass asked with annoyance.

"Facts and history Glass. You said it. I prefer less falling leaves and speculation and more getting on with it. You know this."

"There's not much more. Rosenthal couldn't walk after the beating he took. They put him in the cart being pushed by prisoners who still had the strength. Other men fell, and if they weren't dead they put them in the cart, one on top of the other, at all angles, like a pile of sticks. They were all near death, with Rosenthal at the bottom. He just suffocated under the weight of other prisoners. Even though he was on his stomach his head was twisted up against the side of the cart facing the sky trying to get air. It was no use with all the weight on his body. The agony in his face showed he was alive."

"This you saw?"

"No, I was told by those who were there. Some was in the testimony taken later by the army investigators.

"The burial also an atrocity. Rosenthal died, and so did two others along the way. One a Catholic, the other a Protestant. When they reached a town to stop for the night, the Germans ordered the prisoners to bury the dead. The few prisoners who could, carried the bodies to a church graveyard. The sexton — who knew the war was ending and the Americans might soon be in charge — tried to create a good record for himself. He said we are decent people—no, the testimony was 'God-fearing people,' and we will give these men their rites. He asked one of the gravedigger prisoners the religions of the dead men. The prisoner said these two are Christians, that one a Jew. The sexton said no, no, no, this can't be permitted. The Christians can be buried here, but the Jew can't be interred in consecrated ground. The wolves barked *'Raus! Raus!'* So the prisoners, almost dead themselves, carried Rosenthal outside the walls of the graveyard and buried him next to the road, in a rut of dirt and mud. Later, the investigators took photos of Rosenthal's body when they dug him out. He was on his side curled up, with his vertebrae and ribs protruding, cradled and white in the earth, like a grub or maggot, something less than human. So you see they succeeded."

Fenster did not look up. Again, he crossed something out and sighed. He continued writing, casually, like he was making a grocery list or doodling. He stopped his pen on the page and looked at Glass. "When they dug him up, was he wearing his dog tag?"

"I think this is enough for today."

"Glass."

"You know! You know! you know he wasn't. What does that matter?"

"Calm yourself Glass. This is good. This is progress. For whatever reason, he wasn't. So fine. He can't be blamed. This is enough of Rosenthal. Rosenthal is dead. You are not. We draw a line under Rosenthal. What happened next?" Fenster drew a line across the page and turned it over.

"What's the point? This is old ground." The pain in Glass's chest returned, and he massaged it.

"Have some water." Fenster stood up to pour water from the carafe at the corner of Glass' desk. A rucked, white wing of shirttail hung over his beltline. Close up, Fenster loomed like he had doubled in size since he came into the room. He poured some water and set it on the blotter. He had pink, glabrous hands like a baby. Glass heard Fenster's heavy breathing and saw below his hat where sweat beaded his forehead and pasted damp curls of hair to his temples. Fenster sat back down.

"You still haven't answered my question of what happened to you?"

"Nothing happened to me Fenster, that's the point."

Fenster, the notebook balanced on his lap with the pen lodged in the spiraled metal, arched back in the chair, clasped his hands behind his neck, and tipped his face toward the ceiling, so that all Glass saw was the bottom of his beard and the brim of his hat. Glass knew he was waiting him out.

"Okay. I came back from the war to New York. I had no family but my uncle who I had been sent to live with years earlier on Stanton Street. The letters from my parents stopped and they were never heard from again." Fenster straightened and took up the pen.

"My uncle was a furrier. He was dying by the time I returned. Years of mercury nitrate they used to treat the furs poisoned him. Before I left for the war he shook with tremors from it. When I got back he had lost most of his teeth, and his gums were blue. For days, we sat at the kitchen table drinking tea and smoking. I held his glass and lit his cigarettes because his hands shook so much. I think he hung on just to see me if I made it back. He asked me all about the war and named the places we had family: Minsk, Lodz, Lviv, Bucharest, Budapest . . . He thought I had gone to each place to check. I told him everything I'd seen, except about the dog tag and Rosenthal. He covered his face with his discolored, flaking hands and wept when he realized everyone but us was gone. He had taken care of me best he could and treated me like his own son, but I felt only enough to be kind to him in his last days, and nothing more. He gripped my arm and said 'you are a hero and will carry on for all of us.'

"When he died, the union newspaper, the *Fur Worker*, said he had no known survivors. He left me everything except $100 which he willed to the union 'for the Socialist cause and my worker brothers –THIS WORLD IS A SWINDLE!' At the kitchen table, he dictated this to me and asked that I make sure the *Fur Worker* used those exact words and that they print the last part in 'big letters like I am shouting it.' These were his last words to the world.

"I had what he left me, and my military benefits. I took a job as a stenographer by day and went to law school at night."

Fenster, who was writing again, asked, "What kind of service?"

"What?"

"For your uncle. What kind of service?"

"Graveside and lightly attended, Fenster. In Queens on a dreary day. He's buried shallow and crowded among the plots of other Jews, in the corner of a cemetery near where the LIE and 54th Avenue intersect. Go take a rock and put it down for the furrier."

Glass paused to look at Fenster who clucked and shook his head at this remark.

"Fenster, you know what? I would've cremated him just to avoid the burial, but cremation right after the war — a bit too on the nose wouldn't you say?" Glass snapped with a manic laugh.

"Really Glass, we've been through this. Morbid jokes will not improve the situation. Let's make use of the little time we have."

Unable to get a rise out of Fenster, Glass continued. "I did well in law school, Fenster, toward the top of the class. As stupid and pointless as it all seemed at first, the law steadied me. And because it distracted me and gave me problems to solve, it was also a comfort. I felt the darkness from Europe lifting. During law school, I was hired quickly as an intern at a white-shoe firm. You know white-shoes Fenster? You don't seem the type."

Fenster rolled his index finger in the air to signal go on, and without looking up said, "The drift I get."

"They gave me the job and put me in a nice office with a hale young fellow from Yale. The next day, the hiring partner comes to me and says 'Come with me Green.' He walks me down to the end of a long, carpeted hall. The secretaries, without raising their heads, follow me with their eyes. He takes me into a windowless office with a chair and a desk and says, 'There was a mistake. This will be your office, Green. Had you told me your background we could have avoided this awkward mix-up, but I never thought to ask.' I remember he looked me over and laughed like it was a joke we both could enjoy. 'You had me fooled. I don't think at this stage it would be right to send you off. I'm sure you'll do very clever work. Please keep the door closed as it's unsightly for the clients to see an open office at the end of the hall.'

"And what did I do, Fenster? How about an answer from you just to change the pace?"

Fenster smiled at Glass, his hands steepled over his notebook.

"Nothing? Psh!" He waved off Fenster with contempt, knocking over the water glass. The water pooled around an easel-backed photograph angled at the corner of the desk. It showed a blonde woman and two tow-headed boys at the beach.

Fenster stood and pulled a balled-up handkerchief from his pocket. He picked up the photo and wiped it off. He blotted the water on the desk and handed the dried photo to Glass, who snatched it violently from his hand. Fenster wiped his face and sat back down. He gestured to Glass to continue, but Glass just stared at the photo.

"It was that September that I met Elizabeth. Elizabeth Constance Bower, from Connecticut. I was sitting on a stone bench at Columbia, the sun so bright it bleached the stone nearly white. I was poring through Scott on *Trusts*. She just appeared standing over me. I only knew she was there because suddenly there was shade. I know, I know, Fenster, and Glass mimicked Fenster's graveled voice, '*stick to the essential facts Glass, not stone, sun and shade.*' She said 'that's a serious book.'

"I looked up at her shading my eyes with my hand, '*Trusts?* literally life and death.'

"From there on, we were always together. She was studying art and design. It was unreal, something that had to be a trick, because it was all so easy and perfect. By winter, we were waking up in my apartment at 108th Street. She sipped coffee in both hands, like it was precious, sitting with her knees pulled up on a little bay window seat overlooking the Hudson. From the bed, against the gray light, when she stood in her nightgown I could see the silhouette of her body, her breasts, her hips, her thighs, like a lovely x-ray; and then, through the window behind her, colorless sky and bare winter branches.

"One morning she saw my watch on the night table. A gift from my uncle and aunt, it was inscribed on the back, '*To Charles, From Avram and Esther with love.*'

"She said, 'You're Jewish? I had no idea.'"

Fenster stopped writing. Glass felt the same sharp pain in his chest and now in his side, and he closed his eyes for a moment to let it pass.

"Why aren't you writing Fenster? Shall we cut through it then? Yes, I explained to her, a Jew, from a long line of them, but you are looking at the end of the line. And just as well because it doesn't mean much of anything to me anymore."

"'Why didn't you tell me?' she asked putting down the watch.

"I remember that question and thinking about how to answer. I thought to say you didn't tell me your religion either and would you expect me to ask? Her question of course insinuated that I was hiding that I was a Jew, and in truth there wasn't a minute until then where I thought she knew, so I really was hiding in a way. So how did I answer? As honestly as I could, so she would understand, because I loved her Fenster and losing her would've broken me. I told her about the war, and Rosenthal, and she's the only person I ever showed this to." Glass showed Fenster the dog tag, holding it up for him to see.

"Ha, it's funny— now Elizabeth Constance Bower and Solomon, uh, you have a middle name, Fenster, you know for symmetry?"

"Emmet."

"Elizabeth Constance Bower and Solomon—excuse me—Doctor Solomon Emmet Fenster are the sole secret-bearers of my life. I told her about the windowless office at the end of the hall. She stood in front of the bay window with her back to me, ethereal in the winter light, and I waited for her to speak. She said again, 'I had no idea,' as if she were playing a reel of us together in her mind to see where she had missed the clues. I waited for her to say it didn't matter to her or to walk out, ready for either. But it's never that easy, is it Fenster? No, she suggested a third option, that was as sweet and tender in intent as it was corrosive in effect. She sat next to me on the bed and said she wanted to stay with me, but look at all the pain that something that did not mean much to me, that was not even really me, had caused, and so why not leave it behind? Why not just let it go? 'Cast it off' she said. It would be so much easier for her family to accept and for the children we would someday have to not have this unnecessary burden. And she said, without irony or cruelty Fenster, I assure you, that there was none of my family left to offend. Why go through the pain, she said? She held my face in her soft hands, beautiful, looking like an angel, a guardian angel trying to save me. Offering me a warm bath to sink into and rest.

"And so I cast myself off. Charles Green was gone and Caspar Glass was born. Without a blip in the world. All that remained, were my same initials, as a keepsake to myself. It was surprising how easy it was to change my name and really my whole identity. Elizabeth and I were married in Connecticut, in a beautiful stone church by a stream, where generations of her family had been married and laid to rest.

"My law career succeeded. We had the two boys you see there in the photo. They are now men in middle age, though I have not seen them for years. Everything was perfect like this photo, Fenster, a beautiful wife and two beautiful boys, do you see it?"

Fenster smoothed his beard. "You aren't in it."

"Let me finish. After years, the lie didn't sit well with me. To the world there was Caspar Glass, a successful lawyer, with a beautiful, intelligent and accomplished wife, handsome achieving sons, and a large circle of friends and colleagues. But in fact, Fenster, I was a cipher, and it was all fake. There was no real connection with anyone, and I even started to feel walled off from Elizabeth. The longer the lie went on the more buried by it I felt. Every time I heard, spoke or saw my fictional name I seethed. There were slights and comments that went unchallenged by me for fear of giving something away. Even in my family. One night at the dinner table my older son, 17 at the time, boasted that he held firm selling his baseball glove for $20 to a younger student who tried 'to Jew him down to $15.' His brother snickered, and I looked at Elizabeth whose head was down moving her fork on her plate. I exploded telling him he should know better than to say something like that, and how had I raised such an ignorant, narrow-minded fool. I stormed away from the dining table. Shocked by my anger, both boys later came to me to apologize. But I knew I was growing more and more estranged. That night, Elizabeth said they were wrong, but that my reaction was 'over the top,' and that the way I was behaving with family and friends was going to raise questions. From then on, I lived with an invisible enclosure around me, like I was an exhibit in a museum, but the world for me existed inside the enclosure. I could see them and hear them through a partition, distant and muffled, but I was suffocating in my shrunken space.

"Over time, I begged Elizabeth that we reveal the truth to everybody. I argued it was the only way to save myself and us. The marriage and our family were failing because I couldn't go on with the lie. It was the worst weakness — to be able to tell the lie and then not see it through. But Elizabeth begged me not to. She said imagine what it would mean to everyone that we deceived them. I withdrew more and more. In every comment and slight I would hear or read, I thought if I don't challenge it then don't I condone it? Are the comments just the minor prejudice anyone might have from ignorance, to be corrected over time, or are these the little slips of the mask of civilization that happen before it's torn off completely?

"And then Elizabeth became ill. Cancer. The doctor pointed to shadows on her x-rays. Soon she had terrible, cruel pain. From her bed she touched my face with a trembling hand and we both talked about years ago on Riverside Drive, and she seemed like an angel again, ravaged and older, now in a hospital gown, but she was beautiful like before. She pleaded with me not to reveal our lie, even when she was gone. She didn't want to be known as a liar to her sons, to her family. She said 'we had a good life together, Caspar, and I'm sorry if you feel we built it on a lie, but I loved you and love you still, and I know you love me. Please don't erase my life at the end. For me, please.'

"Of course, I couldn't. And without her agreeing, what would be the point? She died, and the boys moved away. I'm sure I was the distant angry father who was cold to their mother in their eyes, even at the end. The terrible truth, and I'm ashamed of it, is I had little to do with them after Elizabeth died. I'd lost myself."

At this point, Glass bolted up from his chair. He raised up the photo in one hand and in the other the dog tag, which caught his shirt and ripped it. With both arms raised he shouted, "Have you gotten what you need Dr. Fenster! Is it explained now what happened to me! That nothing happened to me! Am I retained?" He dropped back in his chair collapsing his head on his folded arms, either laughing or crying manically.

Fenster stood, slid his notebook into his pocket and straightened his hat.

"We'll speak again Glass. This is progress."

Glass heard Fenster close the door to the barrister's armoire. He didn't hear anything more. The pain in his chest had receded but he felt a tightness in his neck and jaw. Slumped on his desk, he turned his head toward the window. Reflected in the black glass he saw the door to his office, now open, and the faces of Miriam and others living and dead massing at the door to come and redeem him.

BIRTHDAY

At the park, I met a dog, Hank, as tall as my chest.
His tender skin–cloud skin–stretched across his ribs
carried a deep cut trying to heal.
His fur, short and bristled, raised around it in a protective gesture.

Hank's owner (we always know the dog's names before their
humans),
told me Hank had run off the trail in the mountains above our city
and attacked a deer.
The dog, kicked and sliced by the brute force of hooves.

The owner said he didn't know how to stop it, even though he
screamed 'Hank' over and over
through the brush on the rocky uphill hoping his voice would
somehow untangle the situation.
The deer's blood already seeped into the dirt, its body still, by the
time he made it to them.

My own dog, a lithe creature, a shadow, with an intent only to please,
once cornered a fawn.
The hair on her neck raised into a black raincloud as she barked and
barked.
She couldn't hear me frantically calling her name as slender flesh of
the fawn slammed against
the playground fence again and again trying to escape.
In desperation, I walked away with my dog's ball, and only then she

followed me home,
both our heads hung and silent.

At the park tonight,
both the owner and I say goodbye as the sun sets.
We pet our good dogs, instinctual machines of terror,
on their soft heads.

At night, I sleep better when my dog lays
her weight against my body. Both of us dreaming,
sure of what we could be, before waking to the reality of what we are.
.

STILL LIFE

Every six months I go to the oncology ward and sit in a recliner while an IV
    fills my bloodstream
With an expensive medication that kills my T-cells.

Before the Benadryl kicks in, I make an effort to look around the room. All of
    us there with our small bags of chex mix, goldfish, Famous Amos cookies.
    I am a hard poke, they try again and again to get the needle to the vein.
    When I look up, I see an art teacher I had in college. He is smaller now
    than he was then. He does not recognize me, looks past me in my navy
    blue recliner. I've heard he is losing his memory.

He painted still lifes. The objects, an array of items living within the confines
    of a single canvas, speaking to one another across the textured paint. He
    is 88 years old now. The Benadryl takes effect and the last I see of him,
    his feet are up in the recliner, birkenstocks with socks. White turtleneck
    on this August day. He is reading a thick book. His white hair waving
    across his small head. His paintings were meticulously rendered. He also
    painted Bible scenes–cast out women reaching for a hand, a whole host of
    miracles done by healers. Before I am fully asleep, I see him highlighting
    something in the pages.

I dream a drug-induced sleep. I am at the beach with my friend who died
    three years ago. We are scrambling on the rocks above the clear blue
    water. She is skinny because of the chemo, but so strong. I climb the rocks
    behind her, watching her place each foot on the gray stone, worried she
    will slip, but she doesn't. In the dream, it's clear that her time is limited,

that she won't live forever, or even much longer, but for now, we dive into the warm, blue ocean.

I wake to the sound of drowning, a gurgling that is deep throated. A man across the way dabs his throat with a kleenex. He is not old, in a plaid button up, the top buttons undone so he can breathe through the tube in his neck. Another woman pulls a crocheted blanket close around her shoulders. Lots of people in this room do not have hair. I am part of this scene twice a year and feel guilty that somehow, my disease isn't worse, that the clear liquid in the bag above me ensures this.

The painter is gone now, I did not hear him leave. This room, a still life. A bible scene. A brief moment at the end of things and also, at the beginning.

MOST DIFFICULT

ON the first Friday in December, Alan distributed the poetry unit handout to his Senior Honors English class.

Each student must select a poem. In making your selection, you need not limit yourself to the Norton Anthology, although that should provide sufficient material. Each student will read his or her poem to the class, present commentary, and lead a brief (approximately ten-minute) discussion. Along with presentations, students will submit written analyses (three to five pages). Written and oral presentations must address the following:

- *Why did you choose this poem?*
- *What do you most like about it?*
- *What do you think the poet meant to convey?*
- *Please comment on structure and meaning, and how prosody—the meter and sound of the poem—contributes to the poem.*

Mr. Hartschorn will give a "model" presentation (with student discussion) in class next Monday, December 8th. Starting on Wednesday, the 10th, two students will present their poems each day. The schedule of student presentations is as follows: . . .

He delivered a different model presentation every year. He liked to change it to make it fun or relevant; as it might relate to something that had arisen in class, or world events, or just his mood.

This year, it would be about a personal issue. He had recently experienced a great disappointment. Sharing it, he thought, might be an important step in putting it behind him. Not that teaching was about resolving his personal issues, but he thought it might be instructive, while helping himself find closure.

FOR twenty-five years, he'd held fast to his lifelong dream: to be a writer.

Every day, he rose before dawn, scribbling and tapping away in the huddled glow of a desk lamp. After dinner, while Annette sat downstairs reading or watching TV, he was back at it, churning out notes that led to sentences and paragraphs, that might trickle and bump along and join forces and find their way to become sketches, that would one day blossom into stories and chapters and novels. He wrote and re-wrote; scrutinized and restructured; deleted and polished. He submitted. His short story submissions were met with stiff, polite rejections. His agent queries were messages in bottles, flung into grey seas, where they bobbed briefly before slipping under.

There had been occasional bursts of hope; promising puddles of light in the cloud cover. There had been times when he'd felt himself progressing: his voice growing in authority, his scenes coming to life. He'd willed away doubt. He'd renewed his determination with inspirational notes to himself: *Never let anyone take away your dream. Never let anyone tell you you can't.* He'd staggered on, like a wounded soldier in an old war movie.

But now, finally: Enough. He felt his strength giving out. He felt the ground rising up to meet his fall. He was weary; he was so weary.

ON Monday morning, before first bell, Teresa Preklovitch came to his office. Alan had settled in with his first cup of coffee, reviewing notes for his freshman class. He was pleased to see Teresa in the doorway. She was one of the brightest students in his Senior Honors class. He'd had her in Freshman English, and then in her junior year she'd chosen his Shakespeare class for her elective. He'd allowed himself to think that he might be her favorite teacher.

She sat down in the chair at the side of his desk.

There was something wrong. The first words out of her mouth wobbled.

She hesitated. She tried to compose herself and reset, but her chin quivered, her eyes reddened.

Her story came out, slowly at first, then in a dam-release surge.

Teresa was a pianist. Over the weekend she'd played for the State Piano Teachers' Awards Recital. It was a prestigious competition, for advanced students who could supplement their college application materials with performance scores and recordings. Teresa's piece was a Debussy, an *Arabesque*. She had worked diligently in preparation. She could have played it in her sleep. She was a veteran of high-pressure performances, and she carried an astonishing poise and confidence.

Early in the piece, she'd had a memory glitch. She was ready, though; she knew what to do. She found her footing. And then, *another* glitch. This time—probably because she'd never had two glitches in one performance—she simply repeated the section. But she couldn't play through the trouble spot. She repeated again, but could not grope her way back to the familiar path. She'd had to skip ahead, and landed awkwardly in the middle of a passage. After that, she said, her fingers went off the rails. They'd gone off in seizures, plunking on wrong notes with drunken disregard. She'd kept on, with tears streaming down her cheeks, lurching and sputtering toward a finish line.

The comments from the judges were not kind. Her family and two of her best friends had been in the audience.

Alan listened sympathetically. He extended a Kleenex as she buried her face in her hands. He knew better than to tell her it was all right. He understood that it might be a long time before she was ready to believe that.

"I'm such. A *loser*."

The word came out swollen and wet. And even in the presence of her distress, it startled Alan. The Teresa he knew was relentlessly upbeat. Over the years he had marveled at, and then grown accustomed to the brightening skies of her fascinations, her summery splashes of laughter.

He wanted to hug her, but maintained his seated position, leaning forward, elbows on his knees. "Teresa," he said. "You had a bad recital. That does not make you a loser. You are most certainly *not* a loser."

He suspected that she had come to talk, more than she'd come to listen. It was not likely that she'd leave his office with spirits lifted. But it was possible, he thought, that she might be *diverted*. This, then, was his task: If her thoughts could be diverted, it might disrupt the cycle of self-loathing; of rewind-and-replay.

"We start the poetry unit today," he said. "You might appreciate my sample presentation." He'd found his poem. He would present it for discussion, and he would tell them about the passing of his writing dreams. By making it known, by speaking it out loud, the death would be confirmed. Then, he could leave it behind.

She sniffed, and then wiped her nose. "How come?"

He took a deep breath. "Because every person in the world knows failure, or will know failure." He saw the bunched rows in her forehead, the puzzled tilt of her head. He smiled as he checked the clock. "You can tell me—maybe afterward, if you don't want to share it with the class—if the poem speaks to you."

As he walked to his Freshman English class, he was pleased: He'd shifted her thoughts, at least momentarily. In some small way, his failure might help Teresa.

HE had shared his dream only with the workshop instructors and the tiny and remote circle of aspiring writers that served as his writing community. To these people, he owed no explanations, no resignations, no goodbyes. From these groups, he could simply vanish. Which was fine. But it left his surrender feeling . . . unofficial.

He told his wife. "I'm done," he said.

"Okay." Annette was sorting through the mail. She looked up with a puzzled expression. "What are you done with?"

She had always humored him more than she'd supported him. When asked to read a piece he'd written, she'd tried her dutiful best to be constructive. She was a bit pedantic in her suggestions: *show, don't tell . . .* as he sat jiggling his knee, resisting the urge to call attention to his nuanced references and deft descriptions. She had never ranted with him against the short-sightedness and poor judgment of editors and agents and judges. She had never *believed* in him. "You gave it your best," she said. "There comes a time."

His shoulders slumped. The stark words fell like a hard object on bare floorboards.

"Did you expect to become rich and famous?"

Alan had in fact entertained visions. Not "rich and famous" visions; he'd simply allowed himself to imagine that with some modest success might come some . . . boost to the way people thought of him. "I thought I had a chance to get published," he said.

"Getting published," she said. "Is that really what matters?"

He felt himself bristling. Even though it didn't matter anymore.

"What, exactly, *is it* that you want—wanted? Was it all about writing? Or did you want to *be a writer*?"

This sounded like an accusation: as if wanting to be published made him a shallow person. *Come on*, he thought. Getting published mattered. *Of course* it did. It would mean validation. It would mean that he was not alone with his ideas and visions. It would mean that those ideas and visions were clearly spoken, in a voice worth hearing, and they might venture into the world and connect with others in shared endeavor. At the very least, it was proof; it was *knowing*. That you were good enough.

He'd read widely and diligently: literary journals, debut novels, story collections. He had never accepted that the pieces he read there were superior to his. But the reality could no longer be denied. He was a schoolteacher. Nothing wrong with that. But that's what he was, and all he would ever be. He had to let it go. He wondered how long that would take.

ALAN watched his seniors file in. Teresa usually sat in the middle of the class, but today she took a seat in the front row. Alan understood: She wanted to keep her back to the class, just in case. Alan made eye contact; just a brief nod. Then, he rapped on his desk.

His selected poem, he announced, was "Tichborne's Elegy." He came around to the side of his desk and sat on the edge, one foot dangling, the other on the floor. He explained that the poem was written in the sixteenth century, in the Tower of London, by a man named Chidiock Tichborne, on the eve of his execution. It was a lament for life, laden with ache. He read in a careful, repetitive cadence, his voice rising and falling:

I saw the world, and yet I was not seen
My thread is cut, and yet it is not spun
And now I live, and now my life is done.

When he finished, he re-read brief passages, marveling at the imagery. And then, he hesitated.

He'd always wanted his students to look up to him. He'd hoped to serve as an inspiration, possibly a role model. Had he held himself out too loftily? Too knowledgeably?

This was the part of the assignment where he explained his selection. He stood with his arms folded, frowning down at his elbows. Did he want his students to see him as a failure? Did he want them to regard their teacher as a wasted life, surrendering in futility? Why should he go into this? His anticipation of this moment was based on some theatrical, indulgent view of himself, as if anybody cared. Or maybe he thought somebody might feel sorry for him. He thought of Teresa. Just a few hours ago, he'd actually thought that this poem would be relevant to her; that it might somehow help her feel better. Which was absurd. It would make no difference to anybody, in all likelihood.

From the back row, Jackson spoke. "Thank you, Mr. Hartschorn. Very good job," he said, mimicking Alan's familiar commendation. The students exchanged grins: Jackson was the class clown. "Now, please continue," Jackson said. "Please explain why you chose this poem." The class laughed.

Alan had to smile. He pointed his finger at Jackson: *Good one. Got me.* He looked down at the printed words, and then met the class with his gaze. "I chose this," he said, "because I . . . because a good *friend of mine* . . . has recently experienced a disappointment that feels devastating, that feels like failure. Thinking about that, made me think of this poem."

A few hands fluttered. Alan called on Colette, who could be relied on for thoughtful insights.

"So. This guy." Colette adjusted herself in her seat. "He wrote this . . . in a stone cell? I mean, did he even have a pen and paper?"

Alan put his hand up to scratch at the back of his head. He did not know the particulars of Tichborne's writing setup. "Good question, though."

"Brutal," said Ryan. "What crime did he commit?"

Alan set his lips in a tight grimace. He had a vague memory that it was treason, but he could not remember what treasonous offense had been committed. Hands remained up. Questions were earnest. It pleased Alan that the students were interested, but the questions and comments were better suited for history class: Tichborne's cause, the prison chamber, the English government, the method of execution. Along with: What kind of name is "Chidiock"?

He tried to steer the discussion back to the poem. He'd already commented on language and rhythm; he wanted to talk about emotions. Colette offered a question: Was Tichborne writing about the end of his life, or the failure of his cause?

"Okay," Alan said. "What do you think? Anybody."

Students fidgeted and looked at one another.

In the back row, to everyone's relief, Jackson raised his hand.

Alan feigned weary skepticism. "Yes, Jackson."

"So," Jackson said. "This guy wrote this all alone. Probably while chowing on prison porridge or something. So then, what did he do, read it to the prison guards?"

The class laughed.

Alan explained that it was to be sent to Tichborne's wife, along with a letter.

"So, an audience of one," Jackson said.

They seemed more interested in the poet than the poem, but Alan decided to let it go. For, as much as he wanted them to learn how to use and understand sounds and verses and literature, he also wanted to convey life lessons. He strode back and forth in front of them. He could see his students grappling with the idea of dwindling hours, of one final night. "With no expectation of a reading audience," he said, "Tichborne authored a poem." There was a contemplative silence. "Little did he know that it would live on for centuries; that his poem about failure would turn about to be such a triumph. The triumph of a lifetime."

"Yeah, well," one of the boys said. "He didn't exactly get any glory out of it."

"But just the act of writing itself," Alan said. "You have to believe that Tichborne was pleased with his poem. Was it worthwhile?" He felt their eyes on him. He could mine this vein. "What would *you* do, in that situation?" He winged his arms out. "No chance for escape. You can't even commit suicide; unless you can manage that with a quill pen."

There were thoughtful expressions, angled poses. Someone coughed. "I guess there's not much point to anything," Ryan said. "I mean, maybe you just sit there and remember things, but there's not much point to that, either."

Alan nodded as he continued striding back and forth. "Any pursuit, any endeavor," he told them—"academic, vocational, athletic, artistic—just about anything that requires you to apply yourself. Anything. Can be worthwhile, in and of itself." He wiped at the air. "It doesn't have to *lead* to anything." He heard the words leave his mouth and enter the airspace of the classroom. He wondered if he was wandering too far from poetry discussion. But he wanted them to learn to conduct their lives in the moment, without regard for who was watching, who was judging.

Jackson raised his hand again. "Just curious. But did you say this stuff to your friend—your friend of the big failure? Because, well, what did he say?"

Yes, of course: He'd referred to a failure of a *good friend of mine.* Alan took care to not look at Teresa.

"Or—how bad—what was this failure? Can you tell us?" Jackson clasped his hands in mock supplication. "Promise we won't tell."

Out of the corner of his eye, Alan saw Teresa leaning forward, one hand shielding the side of her face. Hiding: *She thinks I'm talking about her.* A tremor of shame shot through him: He, too, was hiding.

"As a matter of fact," he said. He stopped walking. He faced the class with his arms folded, one hand at his chin. "I lied."

He had their attention.

Alan half-sat and half-leaned against the front of his desk. "The 'friend' of this recent failure," he said, "is me." He told them of the swagger of his youth; his certainty that he was going to be somebody. He told them how, for twenty-five years, he'd written story after story, and two novels, without getting a single thing published. How he'd willed himself on, struggled to believe in himself, but how after so many years it was time to concede the futility of it. How he was struggling now to come to grips with the painful fact that he would never be a writer.

"But I have produced a lot of work," he said. "And you know what, I don't care what these editors think." Which was not quite true, but he continued. "I am proud of what I've written." *This* was true. "And I believe that somehow, my efforts have not been a waste of time." He spread his hands. "And if I'd written some formulaic piece of garbage that got published, would I feel better? If I'd gotten published because my grandfather was the chief editor at some publishing house? Would that feel good? I don't think so." He heard a throat being cleared; he heard someone moving a piece of paper. "I don't think so." He thrust his hands in his pockets. "I mean, it hurts. It hurts a lot. But I have to accept defeat here. Telling you this—hopefully—might help me get over it." He looked up. "So, thank you. For listening."

The class sat in frozen pause, looking up at him with dumbstruck eyes.

A few days later, Teresa stopped in at his office. She seemed to be back to her normal self. She wanted to thank him for listening to her rant and cry. It helped, she said, to know that she could be open with somebody. She apologized. She hoped that she hadn't been too hysterical.

Alan smiled. He was happy that she'd turned to him. He was here to help.

"And 'Tichborne's Elegy,'" she said. "That was amazing."

Teresa was scheduled to present her poem on the following Monday. Alan was curious about her selection.

She'd narrowed her choices to two. She'd been interested in a third—by the local poet Marge Rudlinger—but her classmate Colette had chosen the exact same poem.

"I actually met Marge Rudlinger," Alan said. It had been years ago, just after her first volume had been published. He remembered her saying something about persistence, how it didn't always pay off. "But, anyway"— Alan motioned at Teresa to go on.

Teresa smiled. Her two finalists were "Life is Fine" by Langston Hughes, and "Augmented Chords" by Edward Talleson.

Alan tilted his head. Both great choices. But, Talleson? He was intrigued. Talleson was renowned but obscure; not many people read Talleson. In college, Alan said, he'd considered himself a bit of a Talleson scholar. He wondered how she'd come across him.

She'd never heard of him, she said, but she'd seen a biography about him among the new books at the library. She'd leafed through it, and it looked interesting, and when she saw that Talleson was known for poetry as well as prose, she'd looked up some of his poems and found one that she liked.

"Very interesting," Alan said. "I look forward to your presentation."

AT Barnes & Noble he found the Talleson biography prominently displayed. Edward Talleson, dead for more than a decade, had been an acclaimed but enigmatic figure, in his later years reclusive in the manner of J.D. Salinger. His small but devoted following regarded themselves as an esoteric community; they'd read the entirety of his limited but precious body of work, which consisted of two novels, two short story collections, a slim volume of poems, and several dozen essays.

Alan had discovered Talleson in his sophomore year: Modern American Lit. He remembered liking the course reading list, but disliking the professor. Professor Breckens used stoicism to intimidate. His written feedback carried a tone of snide disgust. In class, he felt no discomfort in heavy, ticking silences, all but yawning as the expectations of inadequacy gathered among students trying too hard for the perfect and original comment that might spark an animated response.

And yet, the students hoped to win Breckens' approval. For Breckens seemed to be a man of literary stature. Still in his thirties, he carried an air of tweedy distinction, and maintained friendly relationships with celebrated writers like Dubus and Coover and Talleson.

One of his classmates was unabashed in her disdain: Breckens was a big wannabe, she said. She rolled her eyes. "He kisses up to literary stars at conferences. So he can feel like a big shot."

But that was wrong. Robert Breckens, it turned out, went on to a literary career in his own right, enjoying reasonable commercial success, albeit to mixed reviews.

Alan never read any of Breckens' work, or followed his career.

Despite his dislike for Breckens, Alan loved the class. He devoted exhaustive hours to his final paper, which presented a view of Talleson's characters as proxies for American icons—Emerson, Turner, Whitman—flailing for relevance in the burgeoning suburban culture of post-war America. Alan grew so absorbed in his topic, that almost without effort, he dashed off a short short story, about three pages long, about a callow version of Talleson as a preppy and pretentious 1970s undergrad frequenting a disco. And, when he submitted his paper, he included the story. He hesitated, thinking hard about Breckens' lack of humor and forbidding stares. But he included it. *Screw it*, he told himself. *I wrote this.* It felt good to be bold. He did include a brief note:

This is not part of the paper, but I was having fun and thought this might be good for a grin.

On the day they were supposed to pick up their graded papers, his was not in the box outside Breckens' office.

The office door stood open.

It coursed through his mind that Breckens had deemed his story inappropriate. He stood there paralyzed, wishing he could take back the story, trying to assure himself that it was a simple mistake: Somebody had taken the wrong paper.

Alan rechecked the stack of sealed packets, flicking noisily to signal his presence. Then he knocked, softly. And then again. He obeyed the gruff instruction to enter.

Breckens sat at his desk with his back to the door. Alan waited several seconds.

"Yes." Breckens swiveled abruptly. "How can I help you?"

"My paper," Alan said.

Breckens motioned at the open doorway. "Right there." He turned back to his desk. "In the box."

"I—I just looked," Alan said apologetically. "Mine's missing."

Breckens swung back around to stare at Alan. "And you are?"

"Hartschorn. Alan. Alan Hartschorn."

Breckens found a class list and scanned it with furrowed brow. "Oh," he said. "Come back for it in a week or so."

Okay. Possibilities—all bad—reeled through Alan's mind. "Um. Was there something wrong?"

"Nothing wrong. But it's not here. I sent it to Ed."

"Ed?"

"Yes. Ed."

Alan stood, dumbfounded.

"Ed *Talleson*?" Breckens leaned at him, cartooning sarcastically, with widened eyes and arched eyebrows. "I believe you wrote about him?"

"Yes." Alan stood still. Waiting. Surely there was more. But when Breckens swiveled back to his desk, he understood that he had been dismissed.

ALAN loved the feel of the book in his hands. The texture of the pages, the crackly sound of the spine flexing, the rolled-oats feel to the walled stack of paper edges. He scanned the narrative on the inner flap. He opened to the table of contents. He fanned through the pages, smelling them. He was not quite finished with the book he'd been reading, but he was getting close. Next up, an early Christmas gift for himself: *A Literary Life: Edward Talleson and American Prosperity.*

ANNETTE had heard of Talleson, but had never read any of his work. Alan told her about the college class, and Breckens, and the paper and the short story. He showed her the book. Annette took it and leafed through. Her eyes darted about the liner flap, with its previews of Talleson's troubled early years, youthful transgressions, his heroism as a navy pilot in Korea, his depression and despair and addictions, the attempted suicide, the publicized affairs.

On Monday morning, Alan found the book on the kitchen table. Annette had already left for work, but she'd placed the book there with a yellow post-it note protruding from the pages.

He turned to the page she'd flagged. It was in the latter third of the book, in the chapter about Talleson's relationships with emerging literary figures. On the post-it note, Annette had drawn an arrow to a passage. And there on the printed page, set off in italics, was a letter from Edward Talleson to the emerging writer Robert Breckens:

Your student's paper is very impressive. I am glad that you sent it to me; it was a pleasure to read. I think he might have articulated some of my own thoughts better than I might have. He is a very talented young man. Please give him my best regards.

And by the way, I loved your short story. It's a hilarious riff, full of your trademark wit (you got in a few great jabs at me!). Plus, I find your characterizations insightful (even as I "shake it" under the disco ball). If you'd like, I think I can help you find a home for this. It could be the start of something for you.

Alan received an 'A' for the paper. There had been minimal commentary. Just a few criticisms about stylistic issues, a few check marks in the margins, apparently intended as commendations. There had been no mention of the story. Nothing relayed from Talleson. Alan had chosen not to seek out Breckens to ask about it.

He sat at the kitchen table, looking at the page. Emotions reeled past like cards being shuffled. Cards for anger; cards for despair; cards for vengeance. He might have heard a military jet flying low over the house. He wondered if the dishwasher was running, if it was malfunctioning in some destructive way. But there was only silence. In his head, there was an image of himself by a railroad, very close to the tracks, where the engine and the cars seemed to be hurtling past at frightening speeds. Each car painted in block-lettering:

now what? . . . so long ago . . . you were good enough . . . still a failure . . .
He wasn't sure if it was ten minutes or forty-five. The train passed, leaving
behind a brief disturbance of wind. It was time for work.

IT was Teresa's turn to present her poem. "This is by William Butler Yeats,"
she said. "To a Friend Whose Work Has Come to Nothing."

Alan was not sure whether he was relieved or disappointed that she
hadn't chosen the Talleson poem. As she read, he focused on her phrasing.
Clearly, she'd rehearsed. She kept an even cadence, trying for the just-right
amount of emphasis on rhymes. Over the latter part of the poem, her voice
took on a resolute tone, of heavy steps negotiating a path among boulders:

. . .

Bred to a harder thing
Than Triumph, turn away
And like a laughing string
Whereon mad fingers play
Amid a place of stone,
Be secret and exult.
Because of all things known
That is most difficult.

When she finished, Teresa brushed her hair from her face. "I really liked
this poem," she said. "I chose it because it's about failure, and I had a really
big one recently. I just—I fell apart—I mean I *totally* lost it, in an important
piano recital. It was, like, complete and utter humiliation. I couldn't face
anybody."

Alan jotted notes as she went along.

Teresa continued, commenting on the heavy tread of sounds like *bred
to a harder thing than Triumph*; the visual imagery of *mad fingers playing
amid a place of stone.* Alan nodded in approval.

After taking a few questions and comments, Teresa folded her paper,
creasing it between finger and thumb. "And one last thing," she said. "Another
reason I chose this was that it made me think of Mr. Hartschorn's story last
week. Because I thought about what he said, and it definitely applied to this

poem." She turned away from the class and looked Alan square in the eye. "But I think this poem is more about bravery than it is about failure." She paused, tossing her hair to one side. "And, um. That's all."

Alan stood up. "Thank you, Teresa," he said. It came out unevenly. "Very good job." He started to add something. *Something*. He felt the class watching him; rows and columns of dead-mackerel eyes. He gulped once, to stave it off, but he felt a bad moment coming. He was afraid that his next words might not make it out cleanly. So, he waited. The class waited. He found himself looking down at the scuff marks on the floor tiles. And then, two words croaked forth: "Class dismissed."

From the classroom, his office was just two doors down. Alan entered the stream of traffic in the corridor. He knew that he didn't look quite right; he could feel the heat in his face.

As he unlocked the door, he felt a nudge at his elbow. It was Teresa. He turned on the overhead light and set his briefcase on the floor.

Teresa hugged him. Just lightly. He allowed it. But then there was a moment of near-panic, as he realized that she was holding on to the hug, that she'd moved close against him, that the door was open, that he could smell her hair, that it almost felt like he was young . . . but it passed, a mere shimmer of a moment. Everything corrected itself. She stood back, smiling. "I haven't read your writing," she said. "I bet I'd like it. But no matter what, I'm proud of you. For everything."

"Thank you," he said.

She took her hands from his elbows and put them in her pockets. "Um." She smiled. "I'd better get to calculus."

He stood leaning against the doorframe, watching her make her way down the hall. In that moment, when she hugged him, there had been a momentary stir. It whooshed him back through the tunnel of years, back to his own days in these same classrooms and corridors. It filled him with an autumnal melancholy; both happy and sad.

Before this morning's revelation, he'd been making progress. On acceptance. He'd assured himself that, if he had to be "just" a teacher, he was a *pretty good* teacher; a teacher who cared about his students.

Perhaps they cared about him. Nobody had ever envied him, but he had an okay life. And besides, he reminded himself, he could still *write*. He just needed to let go of the ambition, the *be a writer* part. But that was the hardest part: letting go of the dream; the dream of being somebody.

The ideas would still come. The visions and hanging "what-ifs" would continue their visits, flitting about like swallows and butterflies. There was no need to turn them away. He could write about these things. He could write about the strange, confused feeling that filled him right now. Perhaps he would write something that would make him laugh or cry. If it did, maybe he would have accomplished something. And if nobody else ever read it, that didn't matter. It would be something just for himself. In all likelihood.

TEN REASONS TO WRITE POETRY

One) last night Hunter diced onions and poblano peppers,
finely, then scraped them into a pot of beef. Two)
it smelled of smoked paprika and cumin and my eyes
welled up with the need for metaphor. Three) my eyes
became rivers—not for their current—for their memory.
Four) there were my ancestors who crossed the river
holding a flood in their eyes. Oh how it poured. Oh how
the land was carved into property. Five) how else to talk
about all that is present—the way time gathers itself at
the edge of a knife (in this case, the one Hunter's obsessed
with, the UX-10 model, the one I tattooed on his leg). Five-B)
we cut time into finely chopped units, last night, had dinner
ready by 6:52, which was 22 minutes late or as on time
as ever, and by that point whatever sorrow (river) I had carried
with me to the kitchen had disappeared, because Six) he'd
asked how I was and Seven) he put his hand on my back
and Eight) something about spice and steam in the air
can release a laughter I hadn't known that I'd held,
which calls for repetition—the river—sprang forth,
was called out, from inside the body. That is, Nine) healing
comes even for the bodies who have refused to be bodies.
For even the bodies who cut up the rivers and clenched water
with jaws or fists or dams and there is the way my grandma
taught us that everything could be made right in the kitchen:
all of last week's dinners thrown into the same casserole dish,
which brings me back to the narrative of this poem, the dish
(it can hold everything) in which we rolled the meat in tortillas

and covered them with cheese and canned sauce, Hunter asking,
you think this is enough? as I felt history spill out the side, as if
this could ever be enough, this one dinner, What, for Ten) people?

NORTHBOUND TRAIN TO PENN STATION, 2001

NEW Jersey transit into the city is always busy on Christmas, but just enough seats remain empty on the train so that no one has to stand. Kristin and Wes take a two-seater.

> *The next station is South Amboy. When leaving the train, please*
> *watch the gap.*

Kristin sits in the window with the 2 lb. can of ShopRite yams on her lap. Wes clinks it twice with his wedding band and says, "I still don't think we're bringing enough."

Across the aisle, a woman dressed for church snaps her head toward the metallic sound, places her hand on the boy's leg beside her, then resumes peering peacefully through the window at skeletal trees and spots of week-old snow.

Kristin says, "You really shouldn't play with your ring like that."

"Oh, *come on.*"

"See how nice and clean mine is? Yours looks like you dropped it down a garbage disposal."

"You know that happened once."

The sound of train over tracks is like a boxer working a speed bag. Kristin and Wes listen to the beating.

This station stop is South Amboy. When leaving the train, please watch the gap.

Wes asks, "You really don't think Becca has marshmallows up there?"

"I doubt it."

"I can't believe we're going to have Christmas yams without marshmallows."

Kristin lowers her voice. "Are you going to talk the whole ride up? Everyone can hear."

"No one's listening." Wes points to the woman and boy across the aisle. "See? Besides, it's not like we're saying anything bad."

"Keep your voice down. And don't point."

Wes leans near Kristin's ear and walls his hand in front of his mouth. "Maybe when we get off the train," he whispers, "we can sneak into the drugstore for some jet-puffed—"

Kristin pokes Wes in the gut.

"I'm only saying," Wes continues, "that I like marshmallows with yams. It's not some absurd combination or request."

"Do you *require* marshmallows?"

"No, dear. I require nothing."

"Good, because *nothing* is going to salvage this Charlie Brown Christmas. My sister pours cereal on top of milk. I don't know where she got the idea she can host a full holiday dinner."

"That's why I'm trying to help. I doubt we're the only ones who'd like some marshmallows."

"What do you mean we? I don't give a shit one way or the other."

A conductor comes down the aisle looking for tickets.

"You know," Kristin continues, handing the man two tickets and waiting for him to punch and pass, "I asked her like fifty times if she wanted us to bring anything else, and this was it." She knocks the can with her middle knuckle. "The ShopRite kind."

"But did she actually say not to bring anything else?"

"I'm doing what she asked. I'm doing exactly what she's asked me to do. And that's all I can do. That's all I've ever done. Now isn't the time to do things differently."

"I'm only wondering if she explicitly told you not to bring anything else and if she actually said those words. It's an innocent curiosity."

"But if she asked us to bring yams, and we are bringing yams, then why does anything else matter?"

"It's really an innocent curiosity. I know why she wants the yams, and I want them too, especially on account of the whole family blowing off Thanksgiving this year, but it'd be weird if she had said, *Bring the yams and the yams only*."

"Lower your voice," Kristin says.

"I'm just saying."

"And you really need to let the whole Thanksgiving thing go."

"There was never a better time for the family to get together."

"Maybe."

"The one time your parents agreed to leave Florida. Good luck convincing them to come up here ever again."

Kristin and Wes hear a faint voice rapping song lyrics, but they can't make out the words.

Kristin says, "I would've brought the fudge from The Caramel Shop on 35, the stuff Dad used to get us sometimes. Becca loved it when we were kids, but God forbid I try to make her happy now. You know how she can be."

"I know."

"Everything has to be exactly how she likes it."

"I *know*," Wes says. "I really do."

"What do you mean?"

"I mean, I know what you're talking about. Like that time we went over for dinner and Albert put ice cream in his dirty salad bowl with bits of lettuce and dressing—"

"Sometimes I wonder how they were ever married to begin with."

"She had a fit."

"You know, maybe she just wanted her husband to enjoy his ice cream out of a clean bowl. Maybe she just cared."

Wes looks away for a moment, up the aisle, then says, "What did you think I meant when I said 'I *know*'?"

"I thought you were going to say something like *it runs in the family*."

"You always assume that I'm thinking something bad," Wes crosses his legs and wiggles his foot, "but I'm really not."

The next station is Perth Amboy. When leaving the train, please watch the gap.

"To answer your original question," Kristin says, "the last time I went up there she gave me very strict orders about what to bring and how everyone like Uncle Frank and Aunt Stella and the cousins all had their own little set of instructions. So, in a way, she did tell me not to bring anything else. And it was all in that tone. That Rebecc-*uh* tone."

"*J-uhst the yams.* Like that?"

"Sort of. Like, *Uh, will you puh-leaze stop stretching out my clothes? Smocks aren't exactly in right now.*"

"*J-uhst the yams.*"

"*Yea-uh.*"

"I suppose it's a good sign that she's sounding like her old self again," Wes says.

"That lilt in her voice used to make me cringe."

"But isn't it kind of off that she *does* sound like her old self?" Kristin adds. "Imagine becoming a widow and single mother on the same day, then three months later you're baking cookies in the shape of snowmen and Christmas trees."

"It's her way of grieving. You said she's been wearing Albert's clothes, too. It's all part of the process."

"And she still had their game of backgammon on the kitchen table."

"What do you mean?"

"Didn't I tell you?"

"You don't tell me as much as you used to."

Kristin looks out the window at above-ground swimming pools, one after the other, covered and snowcapped.

Wes says, "You only told me that the last few times you went up to see her, she was wearing Albert's flannels and underwear, and the one time you asked her about it, she told you to make her some coffee."

"There could have been a gun sitting on the kitchen table and I would've been less surprised. I remember thinking it was so strange seeing that backgammon game. I never even knew she liked to play games."

"Who doesn't like games?"

Kristin stares hard at Wes. He sheepishly looks down.

"It was an unfinished game left out on the kitchen table," Kristin says. "I shook the dice in one of the little cups and she freaked out."

"What did she say?"

"She yelled. It wasn't much different from other times when I used to touch her things, but there was panic in her voice. You know, I always thought that if I'd had a little sister, I would have let her play with all my things and use all my clothes. It would've been fun."

"Your sister is nuts about you."

"She eventually told me they had started the game the night before. Albert promised they'd finish it the next day after work. Apparently, it was their routine for years. She says he was a very good player, but she had him on a two-game winning streak for the first time."

"So she was going for a hat trick," Wes says. "I wonder if it's still sitting at the table."

"I wonder if something's wrong with me for thinking it's weird that she's kept it out."

Wes puts his hand on the can of yams, palm up. Kristin takes it and they interlock fingers. Palm to palm, aluminum.

This station stop is Perth Amboy. When leaving the train, please watch the gap.

"To me," Wes says, "it's a bit weirder that she insists on hosting Christmas."

The train lightens. Seats open. Across the aisle, the woman dressed for church grabs her boy by the hand to lead him off the train. His Gameboy drops like a loose brick.

"You made me die!"

A young man takes their place. He wears headphones and quietly mouths lyrics to himself.

"Has she mentioned yet when she's planning to have the funeral?" Wes asks. "I wish she would've let me join you to visit these past few months."

"She hasn't said. I feel like she needs tangible proof that it's true. Like maybe they'll find something of his in all the rubble. I don't know. Seems impossible, I guess. Anyway, I think you remind her too much of Albert, but she's looking forward to seeing you now."

"I look nothing like Albert."

"It's not that," Kristin says. "It's how you guys always laughed at the same things when no one else did. Becca and I would always look at each other when you guys started cracking up about something. Maybe she doesn't want to be reminded of his sense of humor or that my husband is still alive and hers isn't."

"What's it like up there anyway? In the city."

"Let's not talk about it here."

"Why not?"

"Too many people. Let's just sit awhile."

"OK."

They release each other's hands, yet both feel like the timing is merely coincidental.

The next station is Woodbridge. When leaving the train, please watch the gap.

Kristin turns her chin toward Wes's shoulder. "It sounds different."

"What does?"

"The city. It seems louder, but it might not actually be louder."

"What do you mean?"

"If you just listen, you'll find out."

"The question means that I care about what you have to say."

"Of course you do. Why else would we be together?"

Wes waits.

"When you walk onto the city street," Kristin says, "it's hard to tell if things have gotten louder or if you've just become more sensitive to the things going on around you. It's like the sounds have hands. They shake you, and it's hard to place where they're all coming from. And the weather feels different. I know what forty degrees feels like, but it doesn't feel like forty degrees anymore. It feels colder for some reason. And it smells."

Wes opens his mouth to ask a question, but Kristin pinches him.

"You'll be walking along fine then suddenly a gust will hit you in the face and sting. It smells like burning," she says. "Like . . . like . . ."

"A burning frying pan," the young man across the aisle says. The headphones are wrapped around his neck. "Smells like an empty pan that's been left on the stove for a real long time. A cheap-ass pan. Like from one of those stores where you go through the wrong door and end up under a pile of clothes, and you can't tell what's dirty and what's clean, and they try and tell you that the stuff used to go for ten times as much, but everyone knows that shit falls apart after you throw it in the wash one time. Don't go buying food stuff at a clothing store, and don't go buying clothes at a place that sells food stuff. That's a mistake right there. But you put one of those cheap-ass skillets on the stovetop, you set that flame to high and let it sit awhile. Half hour, at least. And that's it right there. That's what all that mess smells like to me."

"I'm not sure I know that smell," Wes says.

"Well, if you get off in the city, you bet your ass you'll taste it." He puts his headphones back on and resumes mouthing lyrics to himself.

Kristin says, "I told you people can hear us talking."

Wes looks up and down the aisle. "I guess you're right. But we can hear them too, so what difference does it make?"

For a moment, they say nothing.

Then Wes says, "You think Albert's flannel still smells like him?"

"I told Becca that the smell will go away faster if she keeps wearing it."

"Would you wear my gray robe if—you know."

Kristin's eyes widen in consideration. "You're wondering if you were dead whether I'd wear your clothes?"

"Exactly."

"Would you wear mine?"

"Absolutely."

Kristin looks out the window again.

"I don't know," she says. "You don't really have an aroma like Albert did. He always smelled like flowers, but not soapy, somehow natural."

Kristin smells Wes, and when their eyes meet, he asks, "What do I smell like?"

"Bread."

This station stop is Woodbridge. When leaving the train, please watch the gap.

"Can I tell you something?" Kristin asks. "It's dumb, but it's been on my mind. I just don't want it to turn into a thing."

Wes stiffens. "I don't want to argue."

"No, no. I think I know why I never ended up telling you about the backgammon thing."

Wes relaxes his shoulders.

"When I saw the backgammon set out on her table," Kristin says, "I wondered again why you and I don't play games with each other, why we don't do activities together."

"That's not true," Wes says. "We watch TV together. We go for walks."

"When's the last time we went for a walk?"

"It's been a while, but we used to go for a walk every weekend. Nice, long walks."

"We've maybe gone on five or six walks ever."

"You're revising again, like you do," Wes says. "That's not the truth. We went on *at least* three long walks this past summer. I can count: the park, the lake, the Belmar boardwalk—"

"OK, *maybe* two."

"Two?"

"Lower your voice," Kristin says.

"Do you intentionally forget these things?"

"Well, we never play any games, and that's what I was getting at."

"You know I don't like games."

"I know," Kristin says, "but I'm not your dad, and just because it wasn't fun with him, doesn't mean it won't be fun for us. I think it'd be fun to play rummy or chess together."

"I suck at chess."

"I could teach you."

"I didn't say that I don't know how to play. I said I'm not any good."

"Neither am I. Maybe we could get good together."

"Why can't you accept this about me? I feel like this has come up every six months for the past five years. I *hate* games. When I was a kid—"

"I know—"

"Maybe you don't," Wes says. "My dad would teach me a new game and crush me at it for weeks and weeks. He demoralized me. I didn't want to keep playing, and he'd make me sit at the dining room table every night after dinner to play chess or checkers or backgammon or bridge or whatever. He taught me them all, and I never beat him once. Not once. Do you know what that sort of training does to someone? Games are supposed to be fun. He turned a thing designed for pleasure into a painful chore. I shiver at the sight of dice."

"You shouldn't let that man dictate what you enjoy now."

"There might not be an easier thing one could say."

Kristin slumps into the seat and turns the 2 lb. can of ShopRite yams on its side. "You like sports, though."

"I like watching sports. Don't ask me to start playing tennis."

"I guess I just think about Becca and Albert sitting at their little kitchen table, drinking coffee and tea, maybe smoking a cigarette—"

"Neither of them smoke. Smoked."

"But I do. It'd be something pleasant for us to do. Maybe we could give it a try."

"Now you want me to take up smoking."

"Maybe Becca will let us play."

"I'm not touching that board. It's not our game to play."

"But the game needs to end."

"Sure, but we aren't the players."

The next station is Avenel. When leaving the train, please watch the gap.

An elderly pair of matching reindeer sweaters appears where the young man with headphones sat.

"Was he right?" Wes asks. "About the frying pan."

Kristin nods.

This station stop is Avenel. When leaving the train, please watch the gap.

The next station is Rahway. When leaving the train, please watch the gap.

"I hope you have some marshmallows," the sweatered old man says.

Kristin and Wes glance across the aisle. The man points to the 2 lb. can of ShopRite yams sitting on Kristin's lap. Wes's face wins a prize. Kristin looks out her window.

"Excuse my husband," the sweatered old woman says. "We didn't mean to upset you."

"Why are you saying that?" the old man says.

"Sorry," Wes says. "We had a long talk about the marshmallows earlier. We're going to my sister-in-law's, and she gave us very strict orders about what not to bring."

"Sounds like a chef with a vision," the woman says.

"That's one way to look at it," Kristin says.

"Why did you say that to them? '*Excuse me,*'" the man says to his wife. "Why did you say that?"

"Oh, quit your bellyaching," she says.

A loud thud from the back of the train causes everyone to contort in their seats. A piece of luggage fell from the overhead.

This station stop is Rahway. When leaving the train, please watch the gap.

Wes voices the start of a word but swallows it. He and Kristin ignore his aborted speech.

"You know, you've always done that," Wes says. "You get these ideas in your head that we're missing something in our relationship, like we don't get along or something. Like a dumb board game is going to change anything. It kind of makes me sad. I mean, how often did you hear

Becca and Albert ever talk to each other? Like *really* talk to each other. I want you to think about it for a minute before you tell me I've got it all wrong, because I can see it on your face. I can see that you've already got what you want to say all figured out, but just think about it. All the times we had dinners with them and when we went skiing at Big Bear that one time. I don't think I ever heard them say more than a dozen words to each other. Think about that night after we all saw that ridiculous play about the barber's magic comb. You and I couldn't stop laughing, and they didn't share a single word about it. You and I talked about that play for weeks. You forget. For weeks we mimicked the barber's dumb accent. The one who sounded like an even more dimwitted Rocky Balboa. *Why don't yous get 'em all cut?* Maybe they played games because they didn't know any other way to communicate. It was always about who could one-up the other, who could win. What do you think about that?"

Kristin's eyes liquefy. They shake like pools during an earthquake.

"No," Wes says. "I'm sorry."

"We forgot the gifts."

Wes puts his hand on Kristin's thigh and her head falls tiredly into his neck. "I don't think Becca will care," he says. "She'll be happy we have the yams."

"Not Becca. I forgot Kelly's gift. What kind of aunt doesn't bring her only niece a gift on Christmas? And on the first Christmas after Albert."

"I think she'll understand. Kelly's a very mature girl."

Kristin slams her wedding ring into the can. "I was so worried about bringing these motherfu*h*cking yams that I forgot it all."

The next station is Linden. When leaving the train, please watch the gap.

The sweaters leave their seats. Kristin and Wes hear new sounds approaching—heavy footsteps and two men arguing. They take the empty seats across the aisle.

They look like brothers, and the older one, with gray hair above his temples, says, "Have a fucking seat. Cool off."

"I'm cool," the young one says, sitting down in the window. He has a baby face, big round cheeks, and a thin line of hair over his lip. His brother takes the aisle, leaving the seat between them empty.

"You've got some balls to storm off like that, T. You're more like the old man every day, I swear. Cause a big fucking mess and slip out the back door while everyone's turned upside down trying to figure out how the whole thing started to begin with. It's every damn time with you. Always something. And I'm sick of it. Like sick-sick. We used to get along, and now all you do is cause me grief. Consider my position for once. You think I like being the one who has to drag your ass back there every time?"

"I'm not going back this time" T says.

"Please, T. Stop doing this to me. I know who our father was. You know who he was. What else do you want? It's changed for *everyone*. Not just you."

"None of it, Vin," T punches the seat between them, "is the truth!"

"The truth? I swear, sometimes I think about how I could murder you and get away with it. I'd like to squeeze that fat neck of yours and watch those big bologna-skin cheeks explode. We're getting off at the next stop and going back."

"I'm not saying sorry to any of them. I don't owe anything to those people back there. They want to keep calling him a hero. That's what makes *me* sick. They can't admit who he really was because then they'll have to take some responsibility for doing nothing about it all those years. Leaving us in that house. How could they? And now our father's some sort of hero to the world, an angel. Do the angels have bones in their closets? The man never even put out a fire, and they're going to etch his name into stone! It's not right, Vin. It's just not right. What he did in that house for all those years can't be taken back. That shit's written. Like the bible says so."

"Skeletons."

"What?"

"Skeletons, not bones!"

"Whatever, man."

Vin moves to the empty seat next to T. He puts his arm over his brother's shoulder. "Listen, I hear you. I really do. And you aren't too far off, but that doesn't mean I won't wring your neck till your head's straightened out. You made Mom cry over her Christmas ham. She's the one person on this planet who did right by us, you chipmunk fuck. I saw her tears fall on the pineapples thanks to you. She's our *mother*, T. Haven't you come to realize what that means yet? You're twenty-four years old and still sleep in the same bedroom where she used to stick a thermometer up your ass to check your temperature. If she wants to pretend the scumbag she was married to was a saint all along, who the fuck are you to say otherwise?"

"She's lying."

"So let her!" Vin returns to his seat near the aisle. "What did I tell you already? You can't win with her. Why would you even want to? Hasn't she been through enough in this life? Jesus Christ and on Christmas. I swear, if you ever—"

"I was just telling the truth, Vin."

"Yeah, and no one wants to hear it."

This station stop is Linden. When leaving the train, please watch the gap.

The next station is Elizabeth. When leaving the train, please watch the gap.

"Listen, you're going to do this for me," Vin says. "OK? You owe me anyway."

"Owe you for what?"

"For not pushing you in front of this train when you were running down the platform."

"You wouldn't've."

"I really wish the thought hadn't crossed my mind. You know, because what does that say about *me*? You think I'm happy about it? We're going to head back to the house, and you're going to make up something real good for why you stormed off. Matter of fact, hey, lady."

"I think he's talking to us," Wes says.

Kristin whispers, "Shut up."

"Yeah, *you*. How much you want for that can of yams?"

Wes says, "What do you mean?"

"I mean, what's your price?"

"I don't think it's for sale," Wes says.

"I'll give you twenty bucks." He takes out a wad of twenties.

"Where'd you get all that cash?" T says.

"This was part of your Christmas gift till you screwed it all up. Twenty bucks, what do you say, folks?"

"I'm sorry," Kristin says. "We really can't. My sister is waiting for us."

"You're kidding me. I'm saying twenty bucks. That's USD, lady."

"We can't," Wes says. "She's got this recipe or something that calls for the ShopRite kind. I personally think it's some sort of nostalgia thing from when she was a kid, between you and me, but if we don't show up with these—"

"Forty bucks."

"I'm sorry."

"Are you really going to turn down sixty bucks? I'm offering you sixty dollars here."

The train begins to slow.

This station stop is Elizabeth. When leaving the train, please watch the gap.

"Are you folks working me? Eighty bucks? Are you telling me you're going to turn down one-hundred-dollars for a can of fucking yams?"

"One hundred dollars?" Wes says. "Maybe—"

"I'm sorry," Kristin says. "We just can't do it."

The train stops.

"Christ. Let's go, T. Get up. *Get up.* Tell me what the world is coming to. We've got planes flying into buildings and now canned goods are worth their weight in gold. Have a merry Christmas, folks."

"You're right, by the way," Kristin says. "Becca and Albert never talked to each other. Not like we do."

"I didn't mean anything by it. It doesn't mean they didn't get along."

"At times, I guess, but not as much as you might think. She's told me a lot over these past couple months."

"Like what?"

"Stuff about their relationship."

Wes waits. Expecting more.

"I actually shouldn't tell you," Kristin says. "I promised her."

"Why'd you bring it up then?"

"I didn't mean to. It's nothing. I need to keep those conversations private."

"Are you talking about the conversations in a general sense or that there's something specific she told you that you can't tell me?"

"Just forget it."

The next station is North Elizabeth. When leaving the train, please watch the gap.

"That's very annoying," Wes says.

This station stop is North Elizabeth. When leaving the train, please watch the gap.

"I'm not asking you to tell me what she said," Wes says, "but is there some sort of secret that you're keeping from me?"

"It's not a secret. It's just that things weren't going well between them for a long time before he died. OK?"

"What's not a secret?"

"There is no secret, Wes. Stop."

"I don't like when you get secretive. You said you didn't mean to bring it up, meaning there was something you had been keeping from me. I don't like that."

"It's between me and my sister. It's not about you."

"Yeah, but you should feel like you can tell me anything even if you're keeping a promise to her."

"I do feel like I can tell you anything," Kristin says, "but I don't feel like I *need* to tell you everything."

"Oh, I know."

"OK, what do you mean by that?"

"I *know* you feel like you can tell me anything even if you don't feel you *need* to."

"You know what?" Kristin shoves the can into Wes's stomach. "You hold these fucking yams."

The next station is Newark-Penn Station. When leaving the train, please watch the gap.

"She told me last year that she wanted to get a divorce," Kristin says, "and she had finally told him a couple months before—you know. He wanted to work it out. She didn't."

"Is it bad to say that I'm not surprised?"

Kristin massages her hands now that they're free of the yams. "No. I don't know. But Kelly overheard them talking one night. She was spying on them, listening in. She must have sensed something was up way before they even talked about it themselves."

Wes nods, keeps quiet.

"She refused to go to school for a week," Kristin says. "Becca finally agreed to counseling and things seemed to be getting better, but I knew it was only a matter of time. She always talked about how nice it would be to move back to Jersey. To be neighbors. I don't know about that, but I never said anything."

Wes drums a sad beat atop the can of yams.

"Poor Kelly. These past couple months all Becca has been trying to do is convince her daughter that she loved her father. She really did, you know."

"Of course she did."

This station stop is Newark-Penn Station. When leaving the train, please watch the gap.

The doors open and new air pushes through bringing in a herd of passengers. It's only standing room now, and Wes pulls his arms in tightly so people nearby don't touch him.

This next station is New York-Penn Station. When leaving the train, please watch the gap.

Wes says, "If Becca is willing to let us, and you still want to play a game of backgammon later, I'll give it a whirl. Don't gloat when you win though. I can't stand a gloater."

The train approaches a clearing and passengers' heads pivot eagerly toward the New York City skyline.

"Here's what we'll do first," Kristin says. "When we get off, we'll go to the drugstore near Becca's house and pick up a pack of marshmallows. I'll put them in my purse. When we get to the apartment, you'll distract Becca, since she hasn't seen you in forever. You'll walk with her into the kitchen, and chat with her for a bit. By the way, she's going to tell you that if anything ever happens to her, she wants us to raise Kelly—"

"Uh, what?"

"I'll say hello to everyone else. The family should be there already, and at the right moment, I'll put the bag of marshmallows next to one of the fruit breads or someone else's presents or maybe with someone's jacket. So, later, when the timing is right—"

"What about your parents? Wouldn't they want to take Kelly?"

"Are you listening to me? When she takes out the can opener to open the yams, I'll gesture over to the area of the marshmallows and casually say, *Looks like someone brought some marshmallows.* I'll say it barely loud enough so someone else hears it and says, *Oh, yeah, you can't have yams without marshmallows.* Then of course someone else will agree, the night being young. And that should do it. That should get you what you want."

Kristin puts her hand on the 2 lb. can of ShopRite yams. Palm up. Wes looks at it.

He takes it.

This station stop is New York-Penn Station. When leaving the train, please watch the gap.

The train comes to a complete stop.

Kristin and Wes merge into the aisle and shuffle toward the door.

"On the ride back," Wes says, "I get the window."

"You could have had it this whole time."

"I didn't want to make a thing about it."

They step onto the underground platform and hear what sounds like a million kids dragging sticks along an infinite chain-link fence, but it's only the trains.

CHRIS BULLARD is a retired judge who lives in Philadelphia, PA. In 2022, Main Street Rag published his poetry chapbook, *Florida Man*, and Moonstone Press published his poetry chapbook, *The Rainclouds of y*. His poetry has appeared recently in *Jersey Devil, Stonecrop, Wrath-Bearing Tree, Waccamaw* and other publications. He was nominated this year for the Pushcart Prize.

ROCHELLE COHEN lives in Silver Spring, Maryland, and photographs the natural world of the Mid-Atlantic.

DEBORAH COPPERUD is a writer and podcaster in Minneapolis, MN. Her work has been published by *Racket, Blue Earth Review,* and *Great River Review,* with work forthcoming in *Defenestration* and *Another Chicago Magazine.* She co-hosts the It's My Screen Time Too and Spock Talk podcasts.

MARK DOYLE is a professor of history at Middle Tennessee State University. He is the author or editor of four books on British and Irish history, most recently *The Kinks: Songs of the Semi-Detached* (Reaktion 2020). He has been a finalist for short story prizes from *Salamander* and *Pithead Chapel,* and his stories have also appeared in *Beloit Fiction Journal* and elsewhere. He is currently finishing a book about John Cale's album *Paris 1919* for Bloomsbury's music book series, 33 1/3.

MICHAEL FONTANA is a retired activist, teacher, and fundraiser who lives in beautiful Bella Vista, Arkansas. Recent fiction credits include *LandLocked* (forthcoming), *Subnivean*, and *Midnight Chem*.

CAL FREEMAN is the author of the books *Fight Songs* (Eyewear 2017) and *Poolside at the Dearborn Inn* (R&R Press 2022). His writing has appeared or is forthcoming in many journals including *North American Review, The Poetry Review, The Moth, Oxford American, River Styx,* and *Witness Magazine.* He has been anthologized in *The Poet's Quest for God* (Eyewear 2016), *RESPECT: The Poetry of Detroit Music* (Michigan State University Press 2020), *I Wanna Be Loved By You: Poems On Marilyn Monroe* (Milk & Cake Press 2021), *Of Rust and Glass* (Volume II) and *What Things Cost: An Anthology for the People* (University Press Kentucky 2022). He is a recipient of the Devine Poetry Fellowship (judged by Terrance Hayes), winner of *Passages North*'s Neutrino Prize, and a finalist for the River Styx International Poetry Prize. He teaches at Oakland University and serves as Writer-In-Residence with InsideOut Literary Arts Detroit.

CONNIE JORDAN GREEN lives on a farm in Loudon County, Tennessee. Her publications include award-winning novels for young people, *The War at Home* and *Emmy* (Margaret McElderry imprint of Macmillan, reissued by Iris Publishing); poetry chapbooks, *Slow Children Playing* and *Regret Comes to Tea* (Finishing Line Press); poetry collections, *Household Inventory,* winner of the Brick Road Poetry Press Award, and *Darwin's Breath* (Iris Press). Her poetry has been nominated for Pushcart awards. conniejordangreen.com.

KALE HENSLEY is a West Virginian by birth and a poet by faith. You can keep up with them at kalehens.com,

HOLLY HILLIARD has a BA from Duke University and an MFA from North Carolina State University. She currently lives in Pittsburgh, PA.

ASHLEY MAE HOILAND is the author of *One Hundred Birds Taught Me To Fly,* published by the Maxwell Institute, and *A New Constellation,* published by BCC Press. She is a finalist for both books in the AML Awards, a finalist in the category of "Spirituality" in the National Foreword Reviews, and nominated for a Small Press Pushcart Prize. She holds a BFA in painting and an MFA in poetry from Brigham Young University. You can find more of her work at https://ashmae.com/.

ROMANA IORGA is the author of *Temporary Skin* (Glass Lyre Press, 2024) and a *woman made entirely of air* (Dancing Girl Press, 2024). Her poems have appeared in various journals, including *New England Review, Lake Effect, The Nation,* as well as on her poetry blog at clayandbranches.com.

EMMA THOMAS JONES also known as E. Thomas Jones, is a bi+ poet from Georgia who holds an MFA from the University of Arkansas. She is a Pushcart Prize Nominee as well as the recipient of the 2018 Lily Peter fellowship and the 2019 C. D. Wright/Academy of American Poets Prize. She has been published in *The Southern Review, The McNeese Review, American Literary Review*, and others. She currently resides in Northwest Arkansas with her partner, Jami Padgett. Find her on Twitter/X @_ethomasjones.

MERIE KIRBY grew up in California and now lives in North Dakota. She teaches at the University of North Dakota. She is the author of two chapbooks, *The Dog Runs On* and *The Thumbelina Poems.* Her poems have been published in *Mom Egg Review, Whale Road Review, SWWIM, FERAL, Strange Horizons,* and other journals. You can find her online at www.meriekirby.com.

ROBERT KOSTUCK is an M.Ed. graduate from Northern Arizona University. Recently published fiction, essays, and reviews appear or are forthcoming in the anthologies *Everywhere Stories*, Vols. II and III, *Manifest West,* Vol. VI, and *DoveTales* Vols. IV—VII; and many print and online journals including *Takahē Magazine, Concho River Review, Louisiana Literature, Kenyon Review, The Massachusetts Review, The Southwest Review, Free State Review, Zone 3, Saint Ann's Review, Bryant Literary Review, Flyway: A Literary Review, Clackamas Literary Review, Silk Road, Fifth Wednesday Journal, Crab Creek Review, Roanoke Review, EVENT,* and *Tiferet.* He seeks an agent for his novel, short story collection, and essay collection, and is currently working on a series of linked science fiction stories.

EDWARD LEES is an American who lives in London. During the day he works to help the environment and in the evenings he writes poetry. His works have been accepted for publication in various journals including *Southern Humanities Review, Moonpark Review, Amethyst Review,* and *Anthropocene Poetry Journal.* He has been nominated for Best of the Net.

TIM LOPERFIDO is a short story writer from New Jersey. As a first-gen and nontraditional student, Tim began his formal education at community college. Many years later, he earned an MFA in fiction from New Mexico State University. Tim now resides in Pennsylvania, teaching writing for Penn State University. His stories can be found in *Grand Journal, Puerto del Sol,* and *The MacGuffin.*

MARGARET MACKINNON is the author of *The Invented Child,* winner of the Gerald Cable Book Award and the 2014 Literary Award in Poetry from the Library of Virginia. Her second book, *Afternoon in Cartago,* won the 2021 Richard Snyder Prize and has been published by Ashland Poetry Press. She lives in Richmond, Virginia, where she leads poetry workshops.

TRAPPER MARKELZ writes from Arlington, Massachusetts. He is the author of the chapbook *Childproof Sky,* a Cherry Dress Chapbooks 2023 selection. His work has appeared in the journals *Baltimore Review, Dillydoun Review, Wild Roof Journal, Greensboro Review,* and *Passengers Journal,* among others. Learn more at trappermarkelz.com

G.H. MOSSON is the author of two books and three chapbooks of poetry, including Family *Snapshot as a Poem in Time* (FLP 2019). His third full length collection, *Singing the Forge,* is forthcoming from David Robert Books in May 2025. His poetry has appeared in *The Tampa Review, Smartish Pace, The Hollins Critic, The Evening Street Review,* and has been nominated four times for the Pushcart Prize. He has MA from The Writing Seminars at Johns Hopkins, and MFA from New England College, and practices law, raises his kids, and dabbles in literature. For more, seek www.ghmosson.com.

RICHARD PAIK lives in Marblehead MA. His debut novel *A Thing or Two About the Game* (Atmosphere Press) was released in 2022.

CALEB PETERSEN is a poet and fiction writer from Lincoln, Nebraska, where he is currently pursuing a PhD in Creative Writing from the University of Nebraska. He has an MA in Creative Writing from the University of Nebraska and a BA in Theology from Colorado Christian University. His poetry has been published in the Summer 2023 issue of *Deluge Journal* and is forthcoming in their Winter 2024 issue. His poem "Washington St." was selected as an honorable mention in the Nebraska Poetry Society 2023 Open Poetry Contest.

AARON RABINOWITZ is a writer of poetry, creative nonfiction, and fiction. He won Meridian's Short Prose Prize and PRISM international's Creative Nonfiction Contest. He has held residencies in British Columbia, California, and Oregon, and was recently a writer-in-residence at the Banff Centre for Arts and Creativity in Alberta. His writing has appeared in *Grain, The Masters Review, The Malahat Review, Cherry Tree, Jabberwock Review,* and elsewhere. You can find him online at aaronrabinowitz.com.

WILLIAM ROEBUCK completed his diplomatic career in late 2020, after 28 years of service in postings across the Middle East, including Baghdad, Tripoli, Damascus, and Jerusalem. He served as U.S. ambassador to Bahrain from 2015-17. For his 2018-20 service in northeastern Syria, Roebuck received the State Department's Award for Gallantry and a Presidential Distinguished Service Award. He was a runner up for The *Missouri Review*'s Jeffrey E. Smith Editors' Prize for Nonfiction in 2021 and a finalist for the same award in 2020. His work has appeared in the *Chicago Quarterly Review, The Missouri Review, The Briar Cliff Review,* and *The Foreign Service Journal*. Roebuck was born and raised in eastern North Carolina and currently resides in Arlington, Virginia. He serves as Executive Vice President of the Arab Gulf States Institute in Washington.

HILARY SALLICK is the author of two full-length poetry collections, *love is a shore* (Lily Poetry Review Books, 2023) and *Asking the Form* (Cervena Barva Press, 2020). Her poems appear or are forthcoming in *Permafrost, Jet Fuel Review, Notre Dame Review, Ibbetson Street, Small Orange,* and other journals. A teacher with a longtime focus on adult literacy, she serves on the Board of the New England Poetry Club. She lives and works in Somerville, MA. (www.hilarysallick.com).

SONYA SCHNEIDER is a poet and playwright with San Diego roots. She has been a finalist for *New Letters* Patricia Cleary Miller Award and *Raleigh Review*'s Laux & Millar Poetry Prize. Her poetry can be found or is forthcoming in *Catamaran, Moon City Review, Naugatuck River Review, Raleigh Review, Rust & Moth, Sky Island Review, SWWIM* and *Whale Road Review,* among others. A graduate of Stanford University and Pacific University's MFA in Poetry, she lives in Seattle with her family..

EUGENE STEIN lives in Los Angeles with his husband and children. His short stories have been published in *Iowa Review, North American Review, Colorado Review, Witness, Catamaran, Gargoyle, Michigan Quarterly Review*, and other journals. His story in *Iowa Review* won a Pushcart Prize, and his story in *Michigan Quarterly Review* was reprinted in *Harper's.*

MICHAEL CALEB TASKER, winner of the Saturday Evening Post Short Fiction Contest, was born in Montreal, Canada and spent his childhood in Montreal, New Orleans and Buenos Aires. He has been published in numerous literary journals including *Glimmer Train, Ploughshares,* and *The Southern Review.* He currently lives in Adelaide, Australia.

ELLEN JUNE WRIGHT is an American poet with British and Caribbean roots. Her work has been published in *Gulf Coast, Glassworks, Gordon Square Review, Hole in the Head Review, River Heron Review, Plume,*

Tar River, Missouri Review, Prelude, Caribbean Writer, Obsidian, Verse Daily and the *North American Review.* She's a Cave Canem and Hurston/Wright alumna and has received Pushcart Prize and Best of the Net nominations.

KIRBY WRIGHT was born and raised in Hawaii. His new book is *American Dreamland* a collection of poetry and prose published by Bottlecap Press.

RICHARD ZABEL's short stories have appeared in *The Atlantic,* among other literary journals. His work has been included in *The Best American Short Stories* collection, in the "100 Other Distinguished Stories" section. He is a lawyer living in Brooklyn, New York, who also teaches law and has written extensively on legal subjects, such as the U.S. terrorism laws.

.